Becoming
THE NEXT
GREAT
GENERATION

*Taking Our Place as
Confident and Capable Adults*

JONATHAN CATHERMAN

Revell

a division of Baker Publishing Group
Grand Rapids, Michigan

Published by Revell
a division of Baker Publishing Group
PO Box 6287, Grand Rapids, MI 49516-6287
www.revellbooks.com

Printed in the United States of America

Library of Congress Cataloging-in-Publication Data
Names: Catherman, Jonathan, author.
Title: Becoming the next great generation : taking our place as confident and capable adults / Jonathan Catherman.
Description: Grand Rapids, Michigan : Revell, a division of Baker Publishing Group, 2020. | Includes bibliographical references.
Identifiers: LCCN 2019046478 | ISBN 9780800736569
Subjects: LCSH: Young adults. | Generation Z. | Change. | Success. | Self-actualization (Psychology)
Classification: LCC HQ799.5 .C38 2020 | DDC 305.242—dc23
LC record available at https://lccn.loc.gov/2019046478

Published in association with the Books & Such Literary Agency, 52 Mission Circle, Suite 122, PMB 170, Santa Rosa, CA 95409-5370, www.booksandsuch.com.

Some names and details have been changed to protect the privacy of the individuals involved.

20   21   22   23   24   25   26   7   6   5   4   3   2   1

Dedicated to my sons, Reed and Cole—
may my ceiling be your floor.

CONTENTS

PERSONAL MESSAGE TO READERS

Way back in 1997, a struggling tech company took a big risk. They spent a bunch of money on TV ads pitching their new "Think Different" campaign. If the ads worked, people might just see them different, buy their computers, and maybe, just maybe, their tech would become popular enough to make an impact on the world. Perhaps you've heard of the company? Apple.

Turns out, the ads did pretty good. Actually, better than good. People loved them. So much so that the company began to be seen as an influencer. Big-time.

It all started with a sixty-second video ad featuring some of the most iconic personalities of the twentieth century. In the ad, Apple challenged people to believe they, too, are crazy enough to change the world for the better. Celebrating the questioning of traditional ways of thinking, they combined a series of short clips of famous disruptors like Albert Einstein, Bob Dylan, Dr. Martin Luther King Jr., Maria Callas, Mahatma Gandhi, and Amelia Earhart. Over their historic black-and-white images, the narrator payed tribute to their brilliance with the famous opening lines, "Here's to the crazy ones. The misfits. The rebels. The troublemakers. The round pegs in the square holes. The ones who see things differently . . ."[1]

I think these words are impressive. They have inspired me so much that I've committed them to memory and heart. Just like how Apple did such a great job of getting us to "think different," it's my goal in writing this book to challenge you to rethink how your generation will change the world. Specifically, you. I challenge you to discover and develop the confidence and character needed to become an invaluable member of the next great generation.

Call me crazy if you want. I'll take it as a compliment. I'm just crazy enough to believe your young, emerging generation possesses more potential to do good in this world than any generation before. More than us Gen Xers. More than your grandparents' generation. More than any and all generations that came before us. Combined. Don't believe me? Please read on and I'll do my best to convince you. Agree with me? Read on and we'll do our best to convince doubters that you can meet and exceed the successes of all the famous disruptors history now calls geniuses.

For you to become the kind of change agents who press the world ahead, you too will have to be crazy enough to start thinking different about what you'll need to succeed. Specifically, we'll need to challenge some old and failing ways of thinking. I won't tell you what to think, but I will challenge you to rethink a few things. Like fixing the growing gap between your young and our older people. Like why stewardship will make you the best leaders in the world. Like why talent might get you noticed, but strength will make you famous. Like how to find the kind of purpose in your life that can make a difference in the world.

I'm both an unusually tall person and a certified dyslexic. This means I've spent my lifetime seeing and thinking about things a little different than most people. This also means I

seldom fit in with the traditional ways most people do things. Turns out I'm in good company. Most creative types see the world through nontraditional lenses and from varying perspectives. This allows us to catch a glimpse of what *can be* and not just what everyone is used to seeing.

What I'm seeing, and what I believe *can be*, is your generation discovering and becoming the kind of influencers in the world that my generation can barely begin to imagine. So I'm choosing to invest myself in rethinking how to set you up for success. How to guide you in becoming the next great generation. Sound a bit crazy? Good. What did Apple say just before totally transforming the world with their technology?

Because the people who are crazy enough to think they can change the world, are the ones who do.[2]

Care to join me?

—Jonathan Catherman

INTRODUCTION

He just said what everyone was thinking. Well, maybe not everyone at the same time, but definitely every teenager has thought it at some time in their life. Considering we all have been there, are there, or will be a teen someday, his words really do speak for the masses. So on behalf of the masses, here's a throwback thank-you to the Fresh Prince for being bold enough to say what we're all thinking—"Parents just don't understand."

More than the frustration of adolescents worldwide, "Parents Just Don't Understand" is also the song title of the second single from the second studio album cut by the hip-hop duo DJ Jazzy Jeff and the Fresh Prince. Pressed onto vinyl way back in the spring of 1988, the release ultimately stacked up triple platinum sales,[1] was selected as one of the top 100 best rap albums,[2] and earned the duo a 1989 Grammy Award for Best Rap Performance. Talk about being tuned in to the voice of a generation!

The songwriting geniuses responsible for speaking our minds were two childhood friends from West Philadelphia, born and raised. Jeffery Allen Townes, aka DJ Jazzy Jeff—or simply Jazz as his friends call him—took his inspiration to spin records from the block parties he attended as a kid.

His rap partner, the Fresh Prince, brought his lighthearted, profanity-free, storytelling-style lyrics to the mic. As of late, DJ Jazzy Jeff has been spinning records and producing music for more than four decades. Likewise, the Fresh Prince has managed to stay behind the mic and on-screen since he first broke into the entertainment biz. In fact, the Fresh Prince inherited the new title as King of the Screen when he ranked in as one of Hollywood's most powerful[3] and bankable[4] stars. Now known worldwide by his real name Will Smith (yes, that Will Smith), the rapper, producer, and comedian is most famous for his strength as an actor. With films cashing in an estimated $8 billion in global box office sales, it's no wonder Will Smith is recognized as true Hollywood royalty.

"Parents Just Don't Understand" spoke lyrical humor with crushing MTV ratings into what young people were all thinking in the late '80s. Yet DJ Jazzy Jeff and the Fresh Prince's performance of an accidental anthem of a generation was not a totally new theme for frustrated teens. More than twenty years before "Parents Just Don't Understand" hit the *Billboard* charts, an English rock band called The Who released a single named "My Generation." In the lyrics of the song's first verse, the troubles of teens in the mid-1960s were captured perfectly. While the band sang, background vocals and millions of young people joined in *"talkin' 'bout my generation."*

Drop back another ten years into 1956. A truly controversial rock and roller enraged older Americans with his hip thrusting, body twisting, and wild abandonment both on stage and off. A nation of young fans, particularly female admirers, lost all control listening to Elvis Presley sing and dance in ways that drove teenagers wild and their parents mad.

What's funny to think about is that the kids who listened to Elvis Presley became the parents of the kids who listened to The Who. Those kids, in time, became the parents of the kids who rapped along with DJ Jazzy Jeff and the Fresh Prince's "Parents Just Don't Understand." And that rebellious generation became the parents of . . . you. Is this beginning to sound like a teen-history playlist set on repeat?

Just like that, one generation later and we're right back to where your parents left off when they were teens. Today you are confronted by the same dilemma earlier generations struggled to address. Parents just don't understand. They don't get how you can like that music, dance that way, and think you are going to make it in the world acting like that.

It's not hard to find fact-citing experts and opinionated haters who truly believe that many of today's youth are "lost." They say that your addiction to technology, unrealistic expectations, and acts of entitlement are leading you to fall asleep on the job—literally. They believe you are squandering your futures and burdening the rest of us responsible people who successfully became adults without the assistance of smartphones. Shade.

Well, I am not one of those pessimistic people and this is not one of those books that hates on your generation.

Limitless Potential

Instead, I believe in your great worth and limitless potential. This book is about coming alongside and guiding you in discovering and becoming all you were created to be. Those of you who also believe in the greatness of your generation are in good company. Sure, there will always be critics. Pay

little attention to them. You are also surrounded by fans who are investing themselves completely in the unshakable belief that you are the next great generation.

Like me, your biggest fans are convinced that to believe in you is to believe in our future. These people are the parents, educators, mentors, and community leaders who take their responsibility and privilege of guiding the next generation seriously. We know your success tomorrow needs our support today. We want you to remember us as builders of bridges between the generations rather than architects of walls that kept us from connecting with each other.

One of the biggest fans of young influencers was the nineteenth-century abolitionist, writer, and statesmen Frederick Douglass. He wisely said, *"It is easier to build strong children than to repair broken men."* His words were spoken with true confidence. Confidence in the belief that if the next generation is pointed in the right direction, they won't get lost when they're old. This means us Gen Xers and Boomers accept the important and fragile task of directing you well. Important because all our futures depend on you. Fragile because it's far too easy to hurt and scare a young spirit.

So how are we going to get this right? There are countless capabilities and character traits to share with your generation. To be perfectly honest, there are times when the thought of guiding you right feels a bit overwhelming. The demands you face today are countless. The constant flow of information, opportunities, distractions, problems, and decisions you face each day seems never-ending. How can we address them all? The truth is, we can't. So instead of me acting like I know how to handle each and every demand placed on your life, I'm going to fess up, admit nobody knows how to do that, and do my best to share resources that will prepare

you to accept any challenge life demands of you. And here's the thing about challenges. Our brains love a good challenge. You know what our brains hate? Threats.

There is a big difference between a challenge and a threat. Such a big difference that one leads to good performance and the other to poor. I bet you don't even have to guess which goes where.

Challenges

We humans are kind of odd when it comes to challenges. We love them. We thrive on them. We push our physical and mental limits with them. We take on challenges, conquer them, and then make up new ones to prove we can outperform the previous ones. No other species on earth regularly creates new and more challenging ways to push their limits. Only people. There is nothing too difficult, too distant, too high, too deep, too far, too close, too new, too old, too much, or too little for us humans to handle. From the dangers of extreme sports to space exploration, the fragility of saving a life to igniting a love life, the challenge of writing good books to righting environmental wrongs, we've proven ourselves willing to take on and conquer any challenge. On one condition. We're prepared.

Threats

We hate threats. I mean we *really, really* hate to be threatened. So much so that our bodies and minds do some crazy things when faced with a threat. Ever heard of the fight-or-flight response? Of course you have, because you've personally

experienced it. From a big dog to a tiny spider, a friendly prank to a family argument, perceived threats flip a switch in you to either stand and fight or turn and run! The fight-or-flight response is your brain telling your body that this is the best way to survive the threat. Basically, you're not prepared enough to ensure a win, but if you don't do something, you're done.

See the difference between a challenge and a threat? A challenge is a competition. A threat is a conflict. A challenge is invigorating. A threat is frightening. You will accept a challenge with the expectation of succeeding. A threat comes with the fear of failure.

We thrive in a challenge. We survive a threat.

DEMAND → PREPARED → **CHALLENGE** → GOOD PERFORMANCE
→ UNPREPARED → **THREAT** → POOR PERFORMANCE

So, what I'll share with you in the chapters to come are ways to prepare yourself to see the demands of life as challenges rather than threats. To do this best, I've prepared some models. Not the kind of models that post perfectly posed and filtered pictures. Not the kind of toy models that break if dropped. I'm talking about models that are structural designs, that represent patterns. As an author, I do my best to present these patterns in ways you can easily understand and expand on throughout your life. Just be careful. The models in this book are not the only ones you will need to succeed. Life is way too complicated to be guided by any single set of written models. Yet in this book, I will share the patterns I believe will best prepare you to take on the kind of challenges only the next great generation will be capable of handling. That's you.

Okay, you say. What are we working with here? Well, I believe there are four important challenges you need to prepare yourself to accept. Each will help you advance in all you do and excel in performance over those who face the same demands unprepared. The good news is, all four challenges can be practiced by anyone. From the youngest to oldest among us. By effectively rethinking the demands your generation faces, I believe you can outperform previous generations. You can do and be even better than us. Here they are, along with a short explanation.

Challenge 1: BUILD BRIDGES

Construct ways to cross the growing gap between the generations.

Challenge 2: PRACTICE STEWARDSHIP BEFORE LEADERSHIP

Demonstrate responsibility and more will be entrusted to your care.

Challenge 3: TRANSFORM RAW TALENTS INTO VALUED STRENGTHS

Work to make the most of yourself.

Challenge 4: LIVE WITH PURPOSE

Fulfill your vision, mission, and goals in life.

Each of these four challenges are timeless. They worked for members of your parents', grandparents', and even your great-grandparents' generation. Yet how your generation will prepare and practice taking on each of these challenges has really changed. The culture of today is much different than when we were your age. This requires us to rethink and update how you prep to thrive in life's many demands. Only,

the results you get will be far greater than they were for us. So, congratulations on that.

As a sociologist, I'm fascinated with the trend of rethinking what worked before in order to work again, in new and better ways. I'll do my best to get you excited about it too. As a parent of two members of your generation, I'm devoted to sharing with my kids every advantage I can without turning them to the entitled dark side. By shining a light on ways of rethinking the following four challenges, I look to lift you all up in a way that you can successfully and effectively pick up, make course corrections, and move onward and upward from where my generation left off. Basically, may our ceiling be your floor as you become the Next Great Generation.

Challenge 1
BUILD BRIDGES

*Construct ways to cross the
growing gap between the generations.*

Chapter 1

THE SPACE BETWEEN US

I didn't know the man, but in that brief moment of mixed emotions, I couldn't decide if I felt worse for him or his teenage son. Why would this man I didn't know tell me such a personal story? Was he hoping to impress me in some strange way? Or was he looking for parenting advice without asking me for it? Had he not listened to a word of the keynote speech I had just delivered?

"... And that's what I'm really afraid of," he said, while nervously adjusting a large ring on his right hand, "that my son is going to break my high school record."

With this final statement, he paused and looked at me for a response. As a parent of teenagers speaking to an audience of fellow parents of teenagers, my first thought was—he totally missed the point of why it's so important to raise up our kids to become even better than us. My next reaction was shock at his triggered anxiety level over his son rising to a position greater than his own. As a father, shouldn't he be hopeful, excited, and even a bit braggish that his boy could soon beat his dad's twenty-five-year-old school record? Of all the student

athletes who had played the game since this man had been in high school, the player most likely to best the school record could be his own son. Not a stranger's son. Not a coworker's son. Not a relative's son. But *his* son. Shouldn't this be something worth celebrating? As a father, what could be better?

Before I could come up with some kind of reply, he added, "You just don't understand how competitive our family is."

Oh, I'm getting a pretty good idea, my mind barked. Thankfully my mouth held its tongue.

He continued, "Sports is all my son and I still have in common. Once he beats me at the one thing I did really well, I'll have nothing more to teach him. You know, you're right about how everything is changing fast. I can't help him much with his homework anymore because I don't understand it. I can't keep up with how he uses technology, and cars . . . well, forget it. They've become so complicated, there's no teaching him how to turn a wrench to fix his car in the garage anymore. The one and only thing we have in common is sports. And it looks like I'll soon be left behind there too."

It turned out he had been listening during my presentation. In fact, he related very personally with my message about the widening gap between the generations. What he was trying so strangely to say was that he feared losing a connection with his son.

Is that what you heard too? Seriously. If you were standing there beside us and witnessed the man telling me his story, how would you feel about what he said? Would you be like, "I feel sorry for the guy. He's facing the fact that he and his son are slipping further and further apart." Or would you say, "Man, let it go. Your time has passed. It's your son's turn to do something great. Something better than you did. How about celebrating with him! You can build a relationship

around his achievements and newfound success instead of holding on to your back-in-the-day memories."

Either way, it's clear the man was standing on the edge of a relevance and relationship gap with his son and he had no idea how to close the distance. With fewer and fewer shared experiences, they couldn't find many ways to relate with each other. And this was probably hurting them both.

Here's what I think. He didn't care about losing his coveted athletic record. He feared losing his son. From his perspective, all that held them together was sports. Their one last father/son connection. Once that was gone, he'd have nothing more to teach his son.

In the last few years, I've noted an increase in similar conversations. I've heard parents, educators, and community and faith leaders each ask their own version of the same two questions. First, "How do we close the gap between the generations so we can stay connected and relevant to each other?" And second, "What can we teach them—today's emerging generation—that will guide them to do and be even better than us?"

Spoiler alert: most of this book focuses on the second of these two questions. But before we go there, it's a good idea for us to talk about the question of closing the gap between our generations. Because let's face it, there's a reason why *Parents Just Don't Understand*.

Moore's Law

The question the adults in your life keep asking me is, *how do we close the gap between the generations to stay connected and relevant?* What they are really asking me is, "How do

we get young people to see things in the same way we adults see the world?"

You may think this question sounds kind of stupid. Most young people tell me they're not too interested in seeing everything the same way as their parents, teachers, and "adult" leaders look at stuff. But from an adult perspective, this is a great question. And like most people, I really like great questions. After all, when you ask a great question, you should expect a great answer. Unfortunately, great or not, most people don't like my answer. At least not at first.

The answer is, *We can't close the gap. You can't get young people to see things like adults see the world. Because Moore's Law makes it too difficult.*

If you are thinking who the what is Moore's Law, you are not alone. After all, who's ever heard of some law that limits how we connect and stay relevant with each other?

Now hold up. Before you start googling this odd law and thinking up ways to protest its lack of inclusion, it's important to know that Moore's Law is not actually a legal law. Instead, Moore's Law is a tech-industry observation and prediction of the future. It was made by a truly geeky computer engineer back in 1965. He just reported what he witnessed, and other people ended up calling his observations Moore's Law. So maybe it would be better if we rebrand Moore's Law as *Moore's Observation*—although I don't believe a name change would make us feel any better, because in the end, the results remain the same.

To help us better understand Moore's Law, here is what the observation is and does, and why it can be blamed for the growing gap between our generations.

Moore's Law was named after Gordon Moore, the cofounder of one of the world's largest microprocessor chip manufacturers.

A few years before Moore and his business partner launched their first company, which later became the Intel Corporation, he worked at another mega-tech company as the director of research and development. As part of his job, Gordon Moore was interviewed by *Electronics Magazine*. In the interview, he was asked if he could predict what was going to happen in the growing tech industry in the ten years between 1965 and 1975. To put this into historical context, that would be right around the same time members of Gen X were being born.

Take a moment to think about what *Electronics Magazine* was asking Gordon Moore to do. At that point in the mid-1900s, the largest corporations and employers included blue-collar automotive, oil and gas, and manufacturing companies.[1] America's tech industry was still in the startup level. Yet many people believed computers were going to become a major part of our everyday lives. Little did they know just how right they were.

Moore knew he had to do his best to get this answer pretty close to right. To come up with his forward-thinking prediction, he paused and took a look back at what had happened in the technology up to that point in 1965. One thing that really got his attention was how (this is going to sound like some old tech-talk here) the number of components in a dense integrated circuit doubled approximately every year, resulting in smaller and faster semiconductors. At the same time, the manufacturing cost per component was dropping. Basic translation = tech stuff was getting smaller, faster, and cheaper.

Moore then turned his attention to the years ahead. He predicted that tech's smaller, faster, cheaper innovation cycle would continue for at least the next ten years. His conclusion was that computers would become powerful enough and affordable enough that almost everyone would soon experience them as part of their everyday life. So Moore submitted his

response in an article titled "Cramming More Components onto Integrated Circuits" for the thirty-fifth anniversary issue of *Electronics Magazine*, in which he said, "Integrated circuits will lead to such wonders as home computers or at least terminals connected to a central computer—automatic controls for automobiles, and personal portable communications equipment."[2]

Yep, his prediction was pretty spot-on. It was like Gordon Moore had stepped into the future, took a look around, went back to his time, and said, "Prepare yourselves! Artificial Intelligence will soon rule the world!"

If you're a little bit confused, it's okay. Components on integrated circuits? What do computer components have to do with the problems kids and parents, students and teachers, young employees and old bosses are having with making personal connections? Well, for me to do a decent job of explaining the effect Moore's Law has had on our relationships, I'll need to tell you a personal story. Don't worry, it's a short one. To set the story up right, try to imagine we are in Seattle, Washington. Just think lots of rain, Starbucks Coffee, and tall green trees. We are at the university I attended, revisiting my favorite professors and one of the most memorable lunches I ever had.

I studied sociology at Seattle Pacific University in the late 1990s. Sociology is the study of society, patterns of social relationships, social interactions, and culture of everyday life. One of my professors was very unusual but a really good teacher. He was a lot younger than most of the university's faculty, lived on an island, commuted to campus on a ferry, rode a fast motorcycle, and was kind of a sushi expert. His teaching style was not normal for the time, as he approached each lesson as more of a guide-from-the-side than as a cringy old sage-from-the-stage. Class time flew by and often ended with

groans from students wishing the talk could continue. To handle both our hunger for learning and need for a midday meal, our professor often invited us to join him for lunch. A short walk across campus and class would unofficially resume in a small restaurant that served really good sushi. Looking back, I believe we probably spent an equal amount of time talking about the development, structure, and functions of human society while practicing the art of eating with chopsticks as we did while taking notes during scheduled class time.

A New Norm

This brings us back to Moore's Law. During one raw-fish-fueled lunch-and-learn, I got to drawing on the back of a soy-sauce-stained napkin. I was sketching a hypothesis that

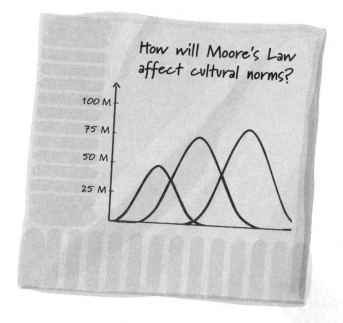

How will Moore's Law affect cultural norms?

combined our studies on generational norms with Gordon Moore's predictions about technology.

One of my line drawings included bell-shaped curves representing the standard distribution of cultural norms in generations past and curves theorizing how future generations would arrange. (That's sociology speak for me drawing a picture that looks like this.)

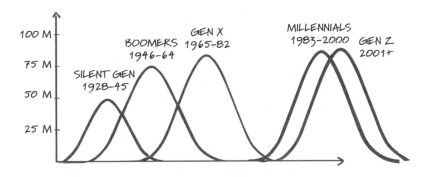

What I drew represented the distance between the peaks of each generation's cultural norm—basically, what each generation thought was "normal" to them compared to what was normal to other generations. The picture ends up showing how much the norms had changed between generations. Look at the distances between the cultural norms of the Silent Generation, Boomers, and Gen X. See how the distances between the bell-shaped curves are even and pretty predictable? But look what happened when I factored in the cause and effect of Moore's Law! (Tech gets smaller, faster, and cheaper.) A new cultural-norm pattern showed up for the generations after Generation X.

Between bites of seaweed-rolled rice and raw fish, we crunched some numbers, did some more sketching, and made

some predictions of our own about how twenty-first-century generations would use technology to interact with information, entertainment, employment, social engagements, and much more. We figured the experiences your generation considered normal would be much, much different than what your parents, grandparents, and great-grandparents experienced. The resulting sketch on the back of a trifolded paper napkin charted a widening of the gap between the cultural norms of Gen X and the following generations we now know as you. Millennials, Gen Z, and the still TBD generations.

Keep in mind when this lunch in Seattle happened. It was just prior to Y2K. Y2K? Sure, then again, none of you would remember back that far, considering you probably weren't even born yet. Basically Y2K is when everyone was losing their minds about how the calendar was turning from the twentieth to the twenty-first century. A lot of people thought that the second after midnight—December 31, 1999—coding wouldn't recognize or register the year 2000. Also called the Millennium bug, lots of people feared that our tech-dependent systems would crash, markets would turn chaotic, and global panic would follow. It was like the world as we knew it *could* come to an end. Or not. The entire Y2K thing ended up being a real bust. A total non-event.

Yep, we really panicked about it. Kind of weird if you ask me, considering all the other crazy stuff we did back then and thought it was fine. Perfectly normal. Like . . . wearing a seat belt in the car was optional. Smoking in restaurants was allowed. Airports had no security-screening checkpoints. America had only been online for a few years, and those who had the internet accessed it through slow, costly, screeching dial-up. At that time, the best cell phones flipped,

the text messaging "fever" was still in its infancy,[3] and we were charged per text message sent and received.

Compare what we experienced then to what most people see as totally "normal" today. Safety belt laws have been enacted nationwide, and indoor smoking is a thing of the past, especially in restaurants. Only ticketed passengers are allowed into airport concourses, and they first have to pass through security checkpoints equipped with scanners and advanced body-imaging technology. And then there's our cell phones. Perhaps it would be better to describe them as pocket-sized computers equipped with social media, gaming, maps, messaging, reading, camera, calendar, web browsing, shopping, and more with every upgrade. Oh, and if truly necessary, they can still make voice calls.

There! We just used Moore's Law to compare your generation with your parents and grandparents. Can you see the distance technology has taken us since they were young? We've come so far, so fast, with so much change. You just became aware of the influence Moore's Law has had on our culture. By citing Moore's Law—yet not by any fault of that law—we can measure with accuracy the unusually wide gap between the cultural norms of twentieth-century generations and your early-twenty-first-century experience.

CONSIDER THIS:

Your generation is far less likely to get the kind of "traditional" teen jobs that previous generations worked when they were your age. Instead, 70 percent of young people today consider themselves self-employed, earning money from a "side hustle" and tech-powered gig jobs.[4]

YOUR TURN:

Compare your experience as a young person with the experiences of members of Generation X or older, when they were your age. What are some of the biggest differences technology made on the everyday experiences of their twentieth- vs. your twenty-first-century generations?

Young people today . . .

When they were your age . . .

- _____

- _____

- _____

- _____

- _____

- _____

- _____

- _____

- _____

- _____

Chapter 2

NEW NORMAL

A little history can really help us better understand this growing gap between the generations. Looking at the norms of the Silent Gen, Boomers, and Gen X, we see that the movement of the cultural norms was slow enough to allow people to share, influence, and pass on many of their life experiences. What was new and innovative for one generation became perfectly normal for their children's generation. For example, let's look at what multiple twentieth-century generations experienced as normal for innovations and improvements compared to that of our twenty-first-century generations. To do this comparison, and for the sake of simplicity, we will track the cultural norm of something very familiar to us all: the telephone.

- Members of the Silent Generation[1] are either the great- or great-great-grandparents of Gen Z. Born between 1928 and 1945, their early memories of making and receiving calls would most likely include

a rotary-dial Bell System telephone. Throughout the United States and Canada, most Bell System subscribers in the mid-twentieth century were connected by shared service lines, popularly known then as a party line. It would have been perfectly normal for members of the Silent Generation to remember the phone occasionally ringing in a coded sequence not assigned to their home. It might have sounded something like "*ring-ring, ring-ring.*" That was the ring code for the neighbors up the hill. The ring code for the neighbors around the corner might have sounded like "*ring, ring-ring-ring, ring.*" Someone had just dialed the other neighbor, yet all the phones on the shared party line announced the incoming call. *(And you're worried about your privacy today. Nobody reads my DM history! Back then people could have listened in on their neighbors' phone calls.)*

- The Baby Boomers are either the grandparents or great-grandparents of Gen Z. They were born between 1946 and 1964 in the era following the Second World War. Many Boomers understand party-line phones as they too experienced them as young children. Advancements in telecommunications shifted the Boomers' normal phone usage to include the spiral-corded, rotary, direct-dial Bell Telephone. Most homes had one phone hanging in the kitchen and perhaps a second sitting on a table in the hall or side room. For the more progressive Boomers, the newest innovation in phones included the touch-tone keypad. For truly advanced phone users, early versions of bulky reel-to-reel answering machines were

cutting-edge technology for the time. Whatever the phone looked like, it was connected to the wall by a cord that carried the conversation through landlines on telephone poles.

- Gen Z's parents are probably members of Gen X, born between 1965 and 1980, and few Gen Xers ever used party-line phones. Those who did probably grew up in outlying rural areas that had yet to phase out party lines. While touch-tone dialing was the norm for Gen X, they also knew how to dial a rotary phone, from personal experience. Gen X's big leap forward included the introduction of cordless home phones, compact tape-recorded answering machines, pagers/beepers, and early brick-sized mobile phones. *(Try this. Ask your parents about pagers. They'll probably say something about how cool pagers were and that all the doctors—and drug dealers—had them.)*

What's important to remember here is how each of the above generations shared many of their life experiences, including the slow progression of improvements in what each considered to be "normal" phone use. A telephone innovation experienced by a limited number of people in one generation becomes the normal phone used by all members of the next generation. What is normal for that generation becomes old technology for the next. Still, all three generations encountered new and improved telephone technology at a similar pace. They shared in the experience.

Then it happened. Moore's Law reached an important and powerful tipping point. Integrated circuits became small

enough, functioned fast enough, and were light enough that, in the measure of a single generation, the cultural norm shifted far enough that the shared telecom experiences of three generations became obsolete to members of the newest, postmillennium generation. The gap that separates twentieth- from twenty-first-century phone use eliminates grandparents and parents from sharing the evolution of phone experiences of most Millennials and Gen Z.

Consider this. Your generation is the first with very limited or no experience in using a corded landline phone. Some of you haven't ever seen and wouldn't know how to dial a rotary phone if you had to. I bet you have never picked up the phone's receiver and dialed "0" to speak to a live switchboard operator. Instead, your normal phone experience includes cell phones that go anywhere; offer unlimited messaging and data plans; stream videos, music, and the internet 24/7; and offer thousands of apps, with updates introduced almost daily.

Pause. Let's look back to my after-class sushi with the cool professor. As unscientific as sketches on soy-sauce-stained napkins appear, it turns out our hypothesis was accurate. Moore's Law really did show how tech would change our view of "normal" between the generations. There is no denying the fact that norms between twentieth- and twenty-first-century generations have fewer and fewer shared experiences. And we're not just talking about our phones. The same growing gap can be seen when we measure other important stuff. Like our experiences in transportation, education, health care, nutrition, housing, entertainment, and the list goes on and on.

After phones, here is one of my other favorite and simplest examples of the drastic shift in what the different generations

see as perfectly "normal." Breakfast cereal. Yes, the first meal of the day has changed big-time in the last century. In 1970 larger grocery stores throughout the United States offered an average of 160 varieties of breakfast cereals to shoppers. By 1998 that number had doubled to 340 distinct options. With new tech powering customization and mass marketing wooing us into buying anything, the number of breakfast cereal options grocery stores could offer shoppers jumped up to 4,945 by 2012.[2] That's a lot of morning meal options to drown in milk. Speaking of milk, in 1970 there was a total of four types. By 1998 shoppers could pick from nineteen variations. Fast-forward to 2012 and consumers had over fifty milk options to go with their 4,945 types of breakfast cereal.

But wait, you might not even drink milk. Not dairy milk, that is. Maybe you prefer dairy-free soy, almond, or rice milk. Not a problem. There's an entire section is the grocery store cooler dedicated to dairy-free and lactose-free milk options. See! Your parents didn't have those options. It's only because of new, faster, and cheaper technology that farmers can even milk an almond or soy bean. Just kidding. (That's a lame Moore's Law "dad" joke.)

But seriously. Consider this mind-bending fact for a long minute. More new technology has been introduced into the world in the last twenty years than gathered in all prior history. That's a lot to learn in two short decades. Good thing we don't have to be experts in all that new stuff. Yes, but you are! Today's youth are the first generation to be "subject-matter experts" on topics of technology *before* their parents.

The order of information sharing used to be that adults taught the youth about the most important parts of life. From life skills to sex education, it was the older who shared

rites of passage and life hacks with the younger. Today, adult supervision is no longer required to learn about almost anything, from about anyone. Moore's Law has resulted in excess access to all topics of information, gathered from around the world, and placed into the palm of your hand. In general, many adults are forced to take a back seat while you teach us how to drive, digitally speaking.

That's just one aspect of the influence Moore's Law has had on different generations. With increased computing performance comes new tech. With new tech comes new and improved products, resources, and opportunities not experienced by prior generations. The result is fewer and fewer shared experiences between the older and younger generations. Thus, stories grandparents and parents tell you that start with, "When I was your age . . ." are heard as ancient history first, and relevant *maybe*.

CONSIDER THIS:

Today's smartphone is millions of times more powerful than all the combined computing power that guided NASA's Apollo 11 to the moon and back in 1969.

YOUR TURN:

1. What do you wish older generations understood better about how things are for young people today?

_____

_____

2. What three things would you like an older person to help you better understand or experience that would make your life better?

- _____
- _____
- _____

Chapter 3

CROSSING OVER

Returning to the question from chapter 1, *how do we close the gap between generations to stay connected and relevant?*

Straight answer: *There is no closing the gap.* Moore's Law does not allow it. But, knowing the shortest distance between two points is a straight line, there is still a way to connect with and share relevance between our generations. Where we can't close the gap, we can build bridges that span the distance between us.

"Okay, we're ready to give that a try," you say. "So, how do we build this bridge between our young and your older generations?" See, that's what I like about young people like you. You aren't afraid to give something a go if you believe it will make a difference. Yet we still have one small problem. I'm not an engineer. Remember, I'm a sociologist. I study groups of people. Not massive construction projects. Then again, you're probably not an engineer either. At least not yet. Now, you and I both know I'm not suggesting we actually

build a steel bridge. What I am saying is, we need to agree on how to construct a way for us to get over the many differences that separate us.

So here's how I think we should start. Let's follow the example of professional bridge builders who managed to span one very wide and dangerous distance between two shores. By using what worked for them as an analogy, we too can bridge the distance between our "old" and "new" shores to accomplish our vision of bridging the gap between our generations.

One of the best bridge-building examples I've found comes from the most famous bridge ever constructed. It's the world's most visited, photographed, and recognizable span. There's a good chance you've seen it in person or driven across from one side to the other. I'm talking about California's Golden Gate Bridge.

When the Golden Gate Bridge opened way back in 1937, it was the tallest and longest suspension bridge on the planet. Boldly painted International Orange, the massive structure stretched out across a one-mile-wide channel. Over frigid cold currents, thick fog, and violent winds that guard where the San Francisco Bay mixes with the Pacific Ocean the bridge is proof that *Where there's a will, there's a way.* Once considered an impossible build, the Golden Gate Bridge now offers easy access between the slower, more rural lands north of the Golden Gate strait and the buzzing hustle of the big city to the south.

For the sake of our bridge-building example, think about the peninsula on the north end of the Golden Gate Bridge—specifically Marin County—as though it represents the older generations that include your parents, grandparents, great-grandparents, and so on. What makes Marin County so

unique is its extremely high biodiversity. The area includes miles of Pacific-swept beaches, rich farmlands, peaceful open spaces, ancient forests, and numerous state parks and natural protected areas. There's a lot of money in Marin County, and the people there are proud of their history, culture, and well-earned influence. Sounds like a good place to represent the generations that came before yours.

Your newer generation is more like the buzz of the big city to the south of the bridge. Perhaps you've heard of the place? San Francisco. A bit different than their neighbors to the north, San Francisco—as both a place and population—is known worldwide for pushing the progressive edge of most every political, economic, ecological, religious, and social issue. Sound familiar? It should. That's exactly what your generation is building a reputation on.

Like in times prior to the opening of the Golden Gate Bridge, the distance between your youthful side of the gap and the older generation's place "way over there" may seem an impossible distance to bridge. Perhaps we, too, think the gap is too great, difficulties too tough, and logistics too many to make meeting in the middle anything more than wishful thinking. That's what some people in both Marin County to the north and the city of San Francisco to the south once believed. That is, until a group of brave and brilliant influencers committed themselves to rethinking what it would take to make building the impossible bridge possible.

Now, if you are really into learning the dirty details about how steel, rivets, and massive cables were united in constructing the Golden Gate Bridge, you are free to Google search and click your way through that mass of research. We're leaving those details out of this book. Instead, what we're going

to do is ask and answer three questions about bridge building that will also help us connect the generations today.

Question 1—Where did they start construction of the bridge?

Question 2—What building materials were used?

Question 3—How did the world know they had successfully bridged the distance between north and south, old and young?

The good news is, each of these questions has a simple and relatable answer we'll use to rethink how we, too, can bridge the space between our generations.

Build from Both Sides

Where did they start construction of the Golden Gate Bridge?

That's an easy one. On both sides. The first step in building the bridge was to construct both the north and south towers. Each tower stands tall and strong in support of the entire weight of the bridge. It was important that both the tower on the northern Marin County side of the strait and the southern tower closest to San Francisco be completed before any of the suspension cables and surface decking could be added. Similarly, for your young generation and our older generations to successfully span any distance between us, we each need to build support on our own side, from our own side.

It's far too easy to point a finger across the gap and say something like, "They really should be doing more to reach out to us." But what good is it to ask the other side to do

what this side is not willing to support? That kind of thinking won't work. What *will* work is for you to start building from your side while we start building from our side. To get both sides doing this effectively, I wrote two versions of this book. In one edition, I focused on writing for Gen X, Boomers, and Silent Generation readers who want to build something great with you. In the other edition—this one—I wrote for your young emerging generation. Each copy presents the same set of tools and models needed to prepare us to see the demand of successfully bridging the distance between us as a challenge and not a threat. Each version focuses on a single end in mind: you gaining access to all you'll need to become the next great generation. For that to happen effectively, we've got to make some important exchanges. So, you start building from your side while we bridge out from our side.

Build to Last

What building materials were used?

Once again, the answer is simple. They built the Golden Gate Bridge with proven materials that would stand the test of time. More than hours, days, and years, the test of time includes all the physical stressors placed on the bridge. Think about it this way. Like the Golden Gate Bridge, the span over the gap between our generations must be built from materials that can stand up to all kinds of pressure. From natural weathering due to the surrounding environment to the massive weight from passing loads, the bridge had to be built from materials proven to last. The real trick was how they joined proven materials together in new ways that allowed them to perform even better than before. So that's

what we're going to do too. Throughout the rest of this book, we will be rethinking how to use proven materials in new ways to outperform previous accomplishments. In the end, we too will be built to last.

Build to Meet in the Middle

What event proved the bridge build was a success?

Again, easy answer. They met in the middle. Two dates marked the magnitude of this event. The first date was on November 18, 1936. On that day, the two center sections of the bridge were joined together halfway between the bridge's main towers. Workers building from the Marin County side in the north reached out and shook hands with workers building from the San Francisco side in the south. A brief ceremony took place at the center of the span before both sides mixed together in preparation of the next important occasion: the opening of the bridge.

On May 26, 1937, the longest bridge span in the world opened to the public. That day more than 200,000 people crossed over the bay waters. Down from the north and up from the south, people met in the middle, mixed together, and moved back and forth over the gap once believed impossible to bridge. Nothing like it had ever been done before.

The only way the two sides were able to meet in the middle is simple: that's the way they planned it from the beginning. When they met in the middle, as expected, those who had done the heavy lifting in constructing the bridge celebrated their success with handshakes and hugs. Then they invited everyone else to join them in experiencing the benefits of

their hard work. The same is true for us. By building in from both sides, with materials built to last, we can meet in the middle, celebrate, and offer passage to others. Just as we planned to from the beginning.

"Okay," you say. "We agree to rethinking the building of bridges. We're ready to start construction . . . from our side, of course. What exactly are we working with here?"

Again, you are asking a great question. For us to get this build right, we'll need to rethink and prepare for more than just building bridges. In fact, I'm asking for a real paradigm shift in how and what you think about leadership, strengths, and purpose. Call me crazy. I'm okay with that. As I wrote in my Personal Message to Readers in the front of this book, I believe your generation possesses more potential to do good in this world than any generation before. But—and this is a big BUT—in order for you to become the kind of influencers who press the world ahead, we must be crazy enough to think different about what you will need to succeed while taking on the challenges of life's many demands. Today's "new normal" is truly unprecedented and requires us all to challenge old ways of thinking about the importance of stewardship, development of strengths, and the significance of purpose.

CONSIDER THIS:

There are over 20 million more members of Gen Z than your Gen X parents.[1]

YOUR TURN:

1. Who are the older people in your life with whom you want to bridge the generational gap between you?

Older People in Your Life

1.   5.
2.   6.
3.   7.
4.   8.

2. From your perspective, what is the level of difficulty you face in bridging the gap between the generations?

(1 = not difficult; 10 = too difficult to consider)

3. Who are the older people you know who are the most willing to collaborate with you to meet in the middle?

_____

_____

_____

Challenge 2
PRACTICE STEWARDSHIP BEFORE LEADERSHIP

Demonstrate responsibility and more will be entrusted to your care.

Chapter 4

RETHINKING LEADERSHIP

There's no way you have made it this far in life without hearing someone say, "Take me to your leader." Early sci-fi movies made the line famous as aliens spoke broken space-English during their first close encounter with earthlings. From TV episodes of the *Adventures of Superman* to the *Teenage Mutant Ninja Turtles*, and songs from as early as the 1950s to just a few years ago, "Take me to your leader" is a pretty well understood request. Basically, "You're not the boss, so step aside and point me in the direction of whoever's in charge around here."

As far-fetched as the special effects in old black-and-white space movies seem today, so goes your generation's views on twentieth-century leadership. Looking back on the model of leadership your parents' and grandparents' generations be-lieved to be high tech, you're probably thinking it's obviously old, outdated, and really pixilated looking. Yet the potential for what the future holds is fresh and exciting to you. So what

does the future of personal and professional leadership look like? Well, following Gordan Moore's example, sometimes the best prediction for what the future holds begins with a brief look back in time.

For years, the generations that came before you worked within a two-layer model that clearly separated the leaders from the followers. Leaders led from above, while followers followed from below. From above, leadership directed businesses, schools, politics, religion, communities, and families. Their position was the reward for workaholic dedication or was boosted through tradition, inheritance, gender, or friends they knew in high places. From below, followers filled lesser roles. Most committed themselves to assigned tasks in the hope of promotion after long years of following orders, gaining on-the-job experience, proving company loyalty, and benefiting from the occasional upper-level job opening.

This top-down, two-layer model was the norm for most members of the Silent Generation, Boomers, and Gen X. Yet the same two-layer model failed to engage Millennials and is widely rejected by the 85-plus million members of Gen Z.

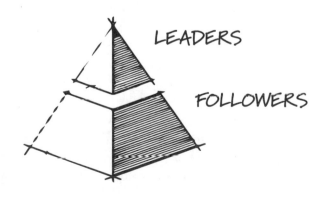

Now that members of Gen Z are coming of age, the combined count of your gen and the Millennial Generation makes for the largest population group in the United States. This means when you demand a change in how people become leaders, your voice can't be ignored. In recent years, your call for an upgraded model of personal and professional development has been heard. Recognizing a model that grants opportunity for anyone to rise to the level of leadership has become both a hot topic and big business. People's willingness to pay for the promise of increased performance has created a highly competitive industry of leadership consulting, coaching, and training.

And that stuff isn't cheap. In recent years, the spending invested specifically in leadership development has climbed into billions of dollars. From large-business management training companies with global offices to focused coaching services that work only with students, it's not difficult to find self-proclaimed influencers willing to sell their solutions for learning the "laws," "levels," "principles," "competence," "effectiveness," and "art" of becoming a leader. To prove the point, try doing a search on Amazon for books that include *leadership* in their titles. You will be overwhelmed with more than 70,000 results, a number that grows daily. So, with all these options, why are researchers still reporting that only 44 percent of high school students are engaged in their learning,[1] 82 percent of work managers aren't very good at leading people,[2] and actively disengaged employees cost the US between $483 billion and $605 billion each year in lost productivity?[3]

Perhaps we are focusing too much on convincing students, employees, and team members that they need to be leaders and not enough on what qualifications they must first steward to make them worth following.

It's no wonder your growing rejection of the leaders-over-followers model begs us to rethink our centuries-old two-layer look at leadership. In the process of redesigning the model, it's still important we don't exclude the common principles anyone can practice in their qualification for the role of leadership. By keeping with what we know works for all generations, the new model will be acceptable and achievable to both pre- and postmillennium generations.

What begins to take shape is an inclusive, three-layer model built upon the qualifications of membership, stewardship, and leadership, obtainable by anyone who chooses a vertical progression to personal development. The conversion from a two-level, top-down model to a three-layer, bottom-up progression requires something that may be difficult for some people to recognize and accept. Leadership is no longer the most significant role one can practice daily. Stewardship is.

Why would stewardship be the most significant of the three layers? Because stewardship is what elevates us beyond the general inclusion of membership and acts as the prerequisite for the role of leadership. Stewardship is particular,

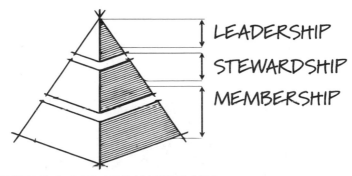

SILENT GEN, BOOMERS, GEN X, MILLENNIALS, GEN Z

long-term, and strengthening. Where membership and leadership both function in public, stewardship is a far more private practice. Stewardship is powered by your personal commitment to integrity, which includes doing the right thing even when no one is watching.

So this means if we are to fully trust those who have risen to the level of leadership to be good at what they do publicly, it's best they are first consistently good at what they do personally. That means the leaders of nations, communities, businesses, faiths, education, sports, entertainment, and our families should first be people of integrity, then popularity.

To establish a strong case for a new three-level layers-to-leadership model, one that requires the practice of stewardship before leadership, let's look into the unique values and differences between each layer: membership, stewardship, and leadership.

CONSIDER THIS:

Gen Z is estimated to represent 75 percent of the workforce by 2030.[4]

YOUR TURN:

1. Where in your own life have you seen the clear two-level separation between leaders and followers?

_____

_____

_____

2. In your interactions with people your own age, how have you observed their displeasure with the old two-layer model of leaders over followers?

_____

_____

_____

_____

3. What are your first impressions of the need for a three-layer model of personal and professional development that includes stewardship as the most important role a person can practice?

_____

_____

_____

_____

Chapter 5

MEMBERSHIP

CAN I JOIN YOU?

Did you know that the earth's population is quickly approaching and will soon exceed eight billion people? That's a crazy-big number. Even more mind-blowing is the calculation made by the Population Reference Bureau that estimates there have been more than 108 billion members of the human race born throughout time.[1] That's an insanely big number.

Consider the diversity of 108 billion different people, each unique in countless ways. Yet evidence suggests one thing has been consistent and shared by us all, throughout history: at our core, all humans share a need to belong to groups. In other words, deep down we all have a basic need for *membership*.

Sure, most people value their independence. Yet no one can live totally independent in and of themselves. Like it or not, we are all members of something. In most cases, multiple somethings. From work to play, worship to education, nearly all human activity is done in some form of group or

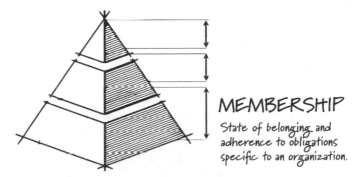

MEMBERSHIP

State of belonging and adherence to obligations specific to an organization.

SILENT GEN, BOOMERS, GEN X, MILLENNIALS, GEN Z

community. Most of these groups are chosen by us, while others come to us naturally.

Chosen vs. Natural Memberships

For example, you can choose if you want to become a member of a health club. So long as you pay the membership fees and follow the club's rules, you'll belong to the group of people who are allowed to exercise in that gym. Your chosen membership is secure. And you don't even have to go. In fact, 80 percent of Americans with health club memberships don't go to their gym regularly.

Other common examples of these member-by-choice groups—we'll call them "chosen" memberships—include subscribers to a YouTube channel, members of a rewards shopping program, attendees at a place of worship, licensed drivers, members of a political party, givers to charity, and followers of someone on social media. If you want to gain and maintain this level of membership, you'll need to commit yourself to at least fulfilling the minimum, often recurring, and usually simple obligations of the group.

Memberships that happen involuntarily—"natural" memberships—are much fewer and usually out of your control. Unlike chosen memberships in which you have a say, natural memberships are selected for you. For instance, no one gets a say in choosing which generation they are born into. Though you may relate better to an older generation or younger age group, your birth date is set and cannot be changed. Likewise, your ancestry cannot be selected. Locked in your DNA is the history of your genealogy. The many characteristics that make you uniquely you stem from branches of your family tree that you had no choice in climbing. True, the choice of who you pass on your genealogy with can be selected. This makes "starting" a family a form of chosen membership. Yet in doing so, nonselected natural membership is passed to your child through their genealogy and generation.

It's important to note that both chosen and natural memberships have their limits. Though natural memberships are more difficult to shed than chosen ones, when the minimum standards of either are violated, you run the risk of losing or being banished from the group.

- Don't pay your gym dues, your membership expires.
- Break the rules of the road, your license is revoked.
- Offend your family's heritage too greatly, you are declared persona non grata (an unacceptable or unwelcome person).

Most people don't like the idea of being separated from a group and will usually fulfill at least the minimum standards needed to maintain their membership. What's also interesting is how our drive to belong crosses societies and eras, as throughout history and around the world, people usually

seek inclusion over exclusion. But why? What benefit does membership offer people? It turns out we like both the physical and psychological benefits associated with membership.

Benefits of Belonging

We each possess the need to belong, and most people do not fare well when that need goes unfulfilled. Those who feel ostracized—deliberately excluded from a group—experience greater levels of stress, confusion, depression, and aggression than people who feel as if they are accepted.[2]

To make matters worse, rejection hurts. Sometimes quite literally. Our neural response to the loss of membership includes heightened activity in two regions of the brain associated with the sensation of pain—the *dorsal anterior cingulate cortex* and *ventral prefrontal cortex*. These areas of the brain work to alert us when we have sustained a physical injury and in response to the negative effects of pain. Studies conducted to measure what the brain registers while experiencing social rejection suggest that emotional suffering can be equivalent to physical pain in its neurocognitive function.[3] What this means is when we feel like we're being purposefully excluded, our brain registers the loss as "painful." This pain can even show up in our language as we describe our feelings as being "hurt." So the next time someone is feeling the rejection of a breakup, being snubbed by a friend, or discovering they were the only one not invited to a party, and they say something like, "It just hurts so bad," they may indeed be experiencing legitimate—though hard to explain—pain.

More than a place to belong, membership also provides us with a semi-safe place to get information, make comparisons, meet to collaborate, get motivated, and find the kind of

accountability we need to stay engaged. Unfortunately, we are also way too familiar with the safety net that membership provides for those who choose to do the least they can while still being counted as part of the team.

For instance, group projects. Have you ever been assigned group work at school where one of your classmates doesn't put in their fair share of effort, or fails to contribute anything of real value, and they still get equal credit? Of course you have. It's annoying just to think about it! And what makes it worse is these slackers exist after graduation too. Coworkers in businesses of all types regularly report frustration with the same less-work-for-equal-credit kind of people. The reason is because when groups increase their membership, the likelihood of loafing also rises.[4] Just standing around looking busy is tempting when compared to the risks that come with offering new and innovative ideas to the group. When blending into the background is a simple and safe way to maintain one's membership, some safe-seeking students and adult "professionals" choose to just go with the flow.

Just doing the least required to get by is the easiest way for you to maintain a position in the slow and often repetitive march through membership. Yet in today's postmillennium gig economy and tech-driven culture, one thing is certain. Nothing in your life will stay certain for long. Whereas the Silent Gen, Boomers, and many Gen Xers had a clear path to security by staying the course and climbing the corporate ladder, that path no longer looks like it once did. Gone are the days of "loyalty gains reward" on both sides of the leader/follower line.

Membership can and will stay the safe place to play for many. With billions of people worldwide working to arrive on the other side of the day safely, membership will forever

remain a crowded space. In fact, you really can't escape membership. Nor should you. It is what keeps us grounded and connected to both our chosen and natural groups. Anyone who believes they deserve to completely leave membership behind has lost touch with where they came from. By separating and elevating themselves with thoughts of being too good for membership, they step back into the old two-level leaders-over-followers model.

Instead, those who participate fully in their membership while choosing to invest in and take care of more than is required of them are choosing to practice acts of stewardship. The addition of stewardship between the old model's "followers" (membership) and "leaders" (leadership) redefines how we grow personally and professionally. Stewardship redesigns the model by becoming the filter for proof of fitness that people must practice before being invited up into the level of leadership.

CONSIDER THIS:

The concept of "third place" is a gathering place separate from home ("first place") and work/school ("second place"). Membership in a third place fulfills our need for social interaction that includes a strong sense of belonging. Examples of third place or chosen membership include clubs, teams, cafés, places of worship, social media, and . . . online video gaming.

1. What are a few groups you have chosen to be a member of over the years?
   Chosen Membership

   • _____
   • _____
   • _____
   • _____
   • _____

   What groups are you naturally a member of, like it or not?
   Natural Membership

   • _____
   • _____
   • _____
   • _____
   • _____

2. What benefits did membership in these groups provide you?

   _____
   _____

3. How did your membership benefit the groups?

   _____
   _____

Chapter 6

STEWARDSHIP

WALK THE WALK

Stewardship, defined as "the responsible management, supervision, and protection of what has been entrusted to your care," is a remarkably private yet revealing trait. True stewards are extremely valuable people. They are thoughtful, respectful, and trustworthy—first with themselves, and then with others. This means stewardship is fueled from within you. You don't need someone else babysitting you along the way, paying you to put in the extra effort, or offering a reward once you're done. This makes the behavior of stewardship a reliable predictor of the value of future performance. It's simple: people who can be trusted with little can be trusted with much more.

The practice of stewardship before leadership establishes a three-level model for both your personal and an organization's growth. Committing to the practice of stewardship

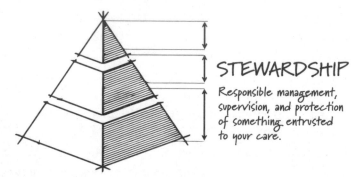

STEWARDSHIP
Responsible management, supervision, and protection of something entrusted to your care.

SILENT GEN, BOOMERS, GEN X, MILLENNIALS, GEN Z

before leadership is an effective way to clarify why, how, and who should be considered worth recognizing as candidates for leadership.

When we look at this three-layer model from the top down, it reveals that the best leaders can be easily identified through their acts of consistent stewardship. Stewardship is about investing in what can be done, and done well, above and beyond the basic requirements of membership.

Consistent stewardship increases one's construct a little bit at a time. Like building blocks, each small act of stewardship stacks together to form a larger structure. If we were to ask which the most important block is, the answer would be, they all are. Individually, they are one-of-one. Together, they can be formed into about anything.

Eventually the time comes when something occurs in your stewardship that causes people to turn and take notice. "How did you do that?" they ask. In a rush to explain the cause of our exceptional performance, we often misattribute it to leadership abilities, when in all reality, such an accomplishment is the buildup of consistent acts of stewardship.

The truth is, you may have been acting as a good steward for some time. It's not like a person at the membership level jumps in a single bound from doing what is expected of everyone to carrying out what only a few are practicing in leadership. You worked up to it by acting with the responsible management, supervision, and protection of what has been entrusted to your care.

Want a real-world example of a teen who is practicing stewardship before leadership? Here's one that got my attention and quickly became a favorite.

Good Eats

I regularly meet and spend time with "wow" people. You know, the kind of people who are committed to making a difference in the world. They talk-the-talk and walk-the-walk as examples of what true stewardship is all about. Most of the time they are adults who have done well for themselves in life and are now turning their attention to doing good for others. They usually have plenty of life experience, lots of influential friends, and loads of money. Now committed to "giving back," their contributions to making the world a better place makes us all sit up and say, "Wow."

Every now and then, I meet a capital "WOW" person. They too talk-the-talk and walk-the-walk of stewardship. But there's something really different about them. The really good kind of different. The "you don't see that every day" kind of different. Like when capital "WOW" is the only word that describes the energetic, quick-thinking, sharp-witted, why-walk-when-she-can-bound, more-empathy-than-is-

legally-allowed, red-hair-visible-a-mile-away teenager with a great laugh. Oh, and did I mention she started and directs a food pantry that racks up the following:

- serves more than 7,000 people every second, third, and fourth Thursday of the month
- delivers fresh produce, nonperishables, and hot meals to senior citizens
- gives school students six weekend meals and two snacks every Friday
- provides children's clothing and professional interview attire for adults
- supplies emergency feeding for first responders and volunteers
- keeps kids from going hungry during the summer break by providing take-home meals for them and their family
- (and more good deeds we'll never hear about)

Yeah, like, WOW!

Mackenzie Hinson describes herself as just another teenager. A teen who believes she is "Stopping hunger, one meal, one family at a time." That's the mission statement she posted on the wall of the Make a Difference Food Pantry—the food pantry she started when she was only ten years old, way back in 2014. Shortly after opening the doors, Kenzie (as her friends and family call her) and her team of volunteers served 937 people. Then 1,287 people walked through the doors the next month. By the time Kenzie was the ripe old age of fifteen, her Make a Difference Food Pantry counted more than 7,000 people served each month.

So what's up with the massive growth in the number of people served? Are more people in Kenzie's community in need? Did Kenzie receive a massive increase in food to give away? Maybe the answer to her growth has to do with how she decided to run the Made a Difference Food Pantry. From early on, Kenzie made it a priority to get to know the people she serves. She learns their names, their stories, their hopes and plans for the future. When people enter the food pantry, they get the feeling they're actually shopping in a market. The space is bright, music is playing, people are talking. The food is fresh, presented on shelves and in displays, and healthy choices are everywhere. Helpful food prep instructions and tasty recipes are available for the foodies, and the kids' room is open for children whose parents need a little break while they shop. And by shop, Kenzie means rolling carts down aisles stocked with ripe fruits, crisp vegetables, fresh meats, and seasonal selections. This is not your typical food pantry. Then again, Mackenzie Hinson is not your typical food pantry founder. Like I said, capital WOW.

But why in the world would a teenager want to commit so much time, energy, money, and care to her community? When the producers of the web series *Returning the Favor* showed up at the Make a Difference Food Pantry asking the same question, Kenzie told the show's host, Mike Rowe, why she does everything with such passion.

"It's fun. It's my life. That's why I do it. It's fun. And you feed people that never knew this stuff existed, and now they do. And you feed 7,000 people a month, it kinda turns into your life, and your love for things. And then yeah, it kinda explodes."[1]

Explodes?! Now that's an understatement. Then again, good stewardship is all about how those who can be trusted

with little can be trusted with much more. So yes, Kenzie's responsible management, supervision, and protection of what has been entrusted to her care has exploded into much more. And "more" seldom goes unnoticed or unrecognized.

Sponsors are a big part of the continued success of the Make a Difference Food Pantry. There's only so much the daughter of a plumber can afford, so when big companies, celebrities, and a small army of mom-and-pop shops and individual donors stood behind Mackenzie, their support clearly said, *We trust you with our money, our resources, our reputation. We trust you to do so much more for your community than we could do alone.* Now that's a powerful compliment about the stewardship of a teenager.

You know what else makes a powerful statement? When the state governor declares April 21–24 "Make a Difference Youth Volunteer Week" and then appoints Kenzie as the state's Spokeskid for Volunteerism. Then there are all the times Kenzie and the food pantry received major donations, cooking and cool-storage appliances, semitrucks of food, giant-size checks, vehicles, media interviews, magazine articles, national news stories, hero awards, and much more by the time this book is released. But to Mackenzie, it's not about the stuff given or attention she receives. It's about how she can do more to care for people in need. She is a master at turning the attention back to multiplying what has been entrusted to her care, to bring more care to others.

Like in Mackenzie's life, you learning how to *practice stewardship before leadership* is key to your current and future successes. Much like the example of people and companies that trust Kenzie to care for her community, any

member of today's Generation Z can practice caring for both their own and others' treasures in a way that demonstrates stewardship—no matter how large or small the value. Mackenzie believes that you can get started now. "You are never too young, too poor, or too anything to get started. You can volunteer in your local community for just thirty minutes a week. All you need is a heart and some time. And everyone has enough of both to share."[2]

Wise advice from a teenager. Notice she didn't say something like, "Go Big or Go Home!" Or "Save the planet and you'll save yourself." Kenzie suggested starting local for a half hour a week. From there, who knows where things will go or how you will grow.

Once again, think of it this way: Those who can be trusted with little can be trusted with much more.

To get us going, let's pick apart our definition of *stewardship*. "The responsible management, supervision, and protection of what has been entrusted to one's care." By breaking down the definition into its individual parts, we can learn a great deal about what stewardship is and why it is so important to your future.

The **responsible** management, supervision, and protection of what has been entrusted to one's care.

> *Responsible*—able to answer or be accountable for something within your control.

The responsible **management**, supervision, and protection of what has been entrusted to one's care.

> *Management*—bringing about success in accomplishing something despite difficulty.

The responsible management, **supervision**, and protection of what has been entrusted to one's care.

Supervision—overseeing performance.

The responsible management, supervision, and **protection** of what has been entrusted to one's care.

Protection—safeguarding from danger.

The responsible management, supervision, and protection of what has been **entrusted** to one's care.

Entrusted—committed or invested with trust.

The responsible management, supervision, and protection of what has been entrusted to one's **care**.

Care—giving serious attention.

For you to truly become the next great generation requires practicing each of the stewardship values listed above. You can't pick and choose the ones you like and the ones you're not willing to commit to.

To set the point, consider the following situation. Pretend you are a young entrepreneur with a really good idea for a great business. But you're not alone. Another person has a similar idea and you two are now racing to find someone to finance your startup companies. You both have a secret solution for solving a very real problem. You both are recognized as rising stars with great potential in your circles of influence. Each of you is asking for $100,000 for a 30 percent ownership share in your company. It just so happens that I have $100,000 and I'm looking for a good business investment. But I can only select one entrepreneur to fund. So let's consider

which entrepreneur best represents the kind of company I'd be willing to risk $100,000 on with my investment.

Company #1—Run by a young entrepreneur who believes in a really relaxed, rule-free, no-need-for-supervision management style. They also have questionable accounting practices and want full control of my $100,000 with no questions asked.

Company #2—Run by a young entrepreneur who demonstrates responsible management of their time and priorities, supervises people and production well, and would protect every cent of my $100,000 like it really was their own.

So, which entrepreneur are you? Which company do you think I'd invest in? The answer is obvious. Company #2 would get the money. And the reason boils down to the increased possibility of your business success and me receiving a strong return on my investment.

Now how about something a little more realistic? Let's face it, I don't have that kind of cash sitting around to invest in a world-changing entrepreneur. What I do have is weekend yard work and a sore back. Upon the painful realization that I can't do the heavy lifting anymore, do I hire the kid down the street to mow my lawn, knowing they don't like to edge and tend to leave behind piles of grass clippings? Would they do an OK job? Sure. I guess. Or, do I pay the kid from around the corner who edges walkways with surgical precision and mows like they are caring for a golf course? Once again, we would all pick the second option. Why? Because of the quality of the lawn care. Even though it's not their lawn, the kid I'd hire would be

the one who approaches the job with great care. This is their practice of stewardship. What starts out as good stewardship of a neighborhood lawn-care weekend job can grow into so much more. Like an entrepreneur seeking $100,000 for their automated, robotic-powered lawn-care service.

Not OK

In early 2019, the AT&T company launched an amusing and memorable series of thirty-second ads. Each ad is set in an everyday situation where the tagline JUST OK IS NOT OK couldn't be truer. The OK Surgeon. The OK Babysitter. The OK brake mechanic. The OK sushi restaurant. My favorite is the OK tattoo parlor. Picture a nervous guy in his midtwenties sitting in a tattoo parlor chair. Preparing to ink the man's forearm is a very chill-looking, smooth-talking tattoo artist who asks the guy if this is his first tattoo. With obvious unease, the man answers, "Yeah." Sounding overly calm, the tattoo artist smiles and tells his customer, "Relax, amigo. It's going to look OK." What follows is a hilarious exchange between the tattoo artist and the man as the poor guy squirms with anxiety, nervously seeking assurance from the artist that his permanent work will look better than only OK. Hearing "No worries, boss. I'm *one* of the tattoo artists in the city" only elevates his anxiety. Doesn't he mean one of the best? Looking down as the work begins, the man is quickly approaching panic as he reasons with the tattoo artist. "Aren't you supposed to draw it first?" The tattoo artist pauses just long enough to look up with a raised brow. "Stay in your lane, bro," he says as the humming tattoo needle pierces the arm of the now regret-ridden guy in his chair.

NO REGERTS

Would you let a just-OK tattoo artist leave a permanent mark on you? You wouldn't? Me either. Why not? Because we might regret it. Same with allowing just an OK surgeon to operate, OK babysitter to watch children, OK mechanic to change car brakes, or OK sushi chef to serve raw fish. For each to be done well requires much better than an OK effort and rating. They each need to be performed by a person who understands that their efforts and outcomes could affect others more than themselves. They each require stewardship's *responsible management, supervision, and protection of what has been entrusted to one's care.* Anything less could end very badly.

Where else do we expect people to practice good stewardship? When we consider the areas of life that affect us, the list is endless. We want banks to be good stewards of our hard-earned money. We look to corporations to be good stewards of the environment. We hope the government is spending every tax dollar wisely. Sadly, we are far too often disappointed with the performance of all the abovementioned. Some people use this as their excuse for not making stewardship the minimum standard for their own conduct. They think, *If big banks, big companies, and big government won't do it right, why should I be held accountable?* And therein lies the problem. Stewardship is not a top-down responsibility. Remember, stewardship is based upon the model that those who can be trusted with little can be trusted with more.

Let's bring the focus back to your generation. How committed are you to stewardship? How prepared are you to

launch into life responsibly managing, supervising, and protecting what has been entrusted to your care? Need some examples? How about your personal belongings, time management, social media, hygiene, driving habits, communication skills, family relationships, friendships, learning, recycling, faith, nutrition, reputation, finances, work ethic, and physical fitness. Just to name a few.

Looking past the here and now, soon you will come face-to-face with even greater levels of everyday stewardship requirements—for example, business, community, family, parenting, and more. And when I say more, well, I'm talking about much, much more. According to the United Nations, your generation is set to inherit the kind of global issues that can only be resolved by international collaboration, followed by sustained stewardship.[3] The list is long, transcends national borders, and holds little likelihood of being resolved before your generation takes over.

Africa	Human Rights
Aging	International Law and
AIDS	Justice
Atomic Energy	Migration
Big Data	Oceans and the Law of
Children	the Sea
Climate Change	Peace and Security
Decolonization	Population
Democracy	Poverty
Food	Refugees
Gender Equality	Water
Health	Youth

Do these issues look a bit intimidating to you? They should. These are the most pressing demands imposed upon vulnerable people and our fragile planet. So the question you now face is, do you—will you—see them as threats you hope to survive or challenges in which you will thrive? The truth of your answer is found in how prepared you are to face each. The only way to prepare to take on the weight of the world is to build up to it.

For you to fully realize your potential and become the next great generation, you'll have to rethink the rise to leadership by committing yourself to *practice stewardship before leadership*. By doing so, stewardship acts as the prerequisite for the quality of leadership you will need to right many historic wrongs and become the next great generation.

CONSIDER THIS:

Popular today with environmentalist and tax-spending oversight committees, the word *stewardship* first appeared during the Middle Ages as a job description for the manager of a large household. Also known as a *steward*, an estate's manager was commissioned with the "careful and responsible management" of property, labor, finances, and the household's reputation.

YOUR TURN:

1. List a few areas of stewardship that have been entrusted to your care.

- _____
- _____
- _____
- _____
- _____
- _____
- _____
- _____

2. In what areas of life do you feel your generation needs to practice responsible stewardship?

_____

_____

_____

_____

3. What acts of stewardship do you feel best qualify a person for leadership in the following groups?

In family: _____

In community: _____

In education: _____

In business: _____

In government: _____

In faith: _____

Chapter 7

LEADERSHIP

BY INVITE ONLY

Leaders are often the ones who see, think, and act different than those around them. In turn, they experience different and often more successful results than others. Yet there are plenty of successful people who see, think, and act different who are *not* leaders. It can be argued that they are instead practicing highly effective stewardship. Their methods of stewardship have produced outcomes that exceed what others are experiencing, but their secret to success remains just that—a secret. These people leave the rest of us behind, scratching our heads and wondering, how did they do that? One thing is for certain: as long as they keep their recipe to success to themselves, they may be "winning," but they are not leading.

So who are the true leaders? In pure dictionary terms, a leader is someone who leads. No shocker there, and not very helpful for what we are working toward. Looking past the basic definition of a leader to the description of what a leader does will help us see more clearly who qualifies for the role.

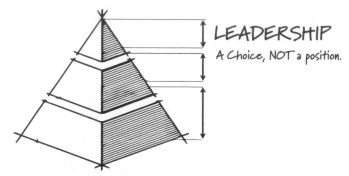

LEADERSHIP
A Choice, NOT a position.

SILENT GEN, BOOMERS, GEN X, MILLENNIALS, GEN Z

Two Great Thought Leaders

Let's start with the thoughts of a couple of powerhouses in last century's leadership development—two guys named Peter Drucker and Stephen R. Covey.

Known as "the founder of modern management,"[1] Peter Drucker had a major influence on the business development and management of countless members of the Silent Generation, Boomers, and Gen Xers.

Drucker's definition of a leader gets straight to the point:

> The only definition of a leader is someone who has followers.[2]

Carve "leader" down to the core and I believe Drucker is right. If you have others tracking along behind you, you are a leader. Where you go, they go. For good or bad, you are their leader. Like these men:

Martin Luther King Jr. had followers = Good
Hitler had followers = Bad

In Drucker's teaching, he wisely separated the position of leader from the act of leadership.

Leadership is lifting a person's vision to high sights, the raising of a person's performance to a higher standard, the building of a personality beyond its normal limitations.[3]

See the difference? Leader vs. leadership. A leader is a ranking while leadership is a role.

Dr. Stephen R. Covey was also a major player in influencing the thinking of leadership in business, education, and personal development. In his words,

Leadership is a choice, not a position.[4]

Now that's an interesting point Dr. Covey makes. By identifying leadership as a choice, he's separating the rank of leader from the action of leading. This means a person can be in the identified position of leader and, at the same time, not contributing anything of value.

Dr. Covey goes on to define the act of leadership in a direct and powerful way:

Leadership is communicating to people their worth and potential so clearly that they come to see it in themselves.[5]

Again, the point is made that there is a difference between the ranking of a leader and the role of leadership. Where the title of "leader" can be given to anyone, the fulfillment of "leadership" is proven by a person's actions—the ability of "communicating to people their worth and potential so clearly that they come to see it in themselves."

Believing strongly that leadership roles should be made accessible to all, from the oldest to the youngest among us, I'm always searching for youth in leadership roles. While conducting research and trainings in Florida, I had the privilege of witnessing a simple yet profound growth in a student who advanced quickly from membership through stewardship and into leadership at his school. With a mentor acting as a guide, the young boy discovered how seemingly small acts of stewardship invited him into the role of leadership and made a real difference in his small south Florida elementary school.

THE CUSTODIAN'S ASSISTANT

Packing up and moving has been identified as one of the top stressors a person will experience in life. Moving and then starting in a new school, midyear, can really kick the stress levels up for young students. Especially when the new school's grade-level structure places a boy who was previously an intermediate student back into an elementary school building. Increase his stress level even more as kids talk about how much bigger he is than most of his new fifth-grade classmates. Some said his size made him look older and tougher, maybe even like a bully. But he knew he wasn't a bully. Just a big kid in a new school. Maybe that's why he kept to himself during lunch those first few weeks. That is, until Mr. Mario, the school's custodian, befriended the gentle giant.

Luis was sitting and eating by himself when Mr. Mario entered the "cafetorium" to begin his after-lunch conversion of the cafeteria back into an auditorium. Maybe his old shoulder was aching a bit more than usual that day or perhaps he saw an opportunity to encourage young Luis; either way, Mr. Mario stopped and asked the new student

if he wouldn't mind helping him move a couple of benches. Without hesitation, Luis got up from his otherwise empty table and assisted the smiling custodian in the task. After learning his name, grade level, and that he was new to the school, Mr. Mario complimented Luis on his willingness to help, his unusual physical strength, and how quick he was to learn the cafetorium conversion process. He told Luis that he was obviously a strong, kind, and smart young man. Then the wise custodian made a casual comment about how maybe Luis could be the first official member of the newly formed cafeteria clean-up team. But only if he wanted to be.

The next day, Mr. Mario returned to the cafetorium to again transform the room after lunch. To his surprise, Luis had already cleared several of the empty tables. Without much to say, the two worked together and completed the task in half the time. Each table cleaned, folded, and neatly moved to the side before Luis returned to class.

The following week Mr. Mario and Luis repeated the task of wiping down, folding up, and stowing away the tables and benches after lunch. Yet something had changed. Maybe it was the sense of pride and ownership Luis felt for his new role. Or maybe it was the feeling of responsibility and comradery that came with Mr. Mario suggesting Luis consider inviting a few more students to join their crew. Much like Luis, the new team members welcomed the opportunity to belong to a group, learn something new, and contribute to an important part of the school day. Several of the new team members were larger boys whose physical size could be intimidating to smaller students. But their hearts were big too, filled with kindness and a willingness to assist in the after-lunch duties once performed alone by Mr. Mario. Besides, who wouldn't want to follow the lead of a kid who enjoyed serving others, included those who felt excluded, knew what he was doing, and was quick to share both what he knew and all the compliments for a job well done. It didn't take long before the crew was calling Luis *Gran Jefe* (Spanish for "Big Boss").

In the weeks that followed, more members joined the after-lunch clean-up bunch. Not all the kids stuck with the responsibility, yet those who did took pride in their work. Their commitment to do what few others did began to change things at lunchtime, and their efforts did not go unnoticed. The cafetorium had never looked better, sounded calmer, or been so orderly. All under the consistent stewardship and encouraging leadership of Luis.

Then it happened. An after-lunch special event was scheduled in the cafetorium. This made that day's conversion from cafeteria to auditorium all the more important. On the agenda, the city's mayor would be presenting an award to one member of the student body who had demonstrated outstanding stewardship at a level other students at the school wanted to follow.

Midway through the assembly, Luis was asked to rise to the occasion, again. This time he was asked to walk from where he sat with his class to stand on the stage, beside the mayor, and accept an award before his classmates, teachers, and community. In recognition as an outstanding member of the student body, for his stewardship of citizenship in their proud city, and for the example he set for others in his leadership role, Luis delivered a confident handshake to the mayor, was given a Jr. Key to the City, and received a standing ovation.

I have told the Custodian's Assistant story hundreds of times to audiences around the world. Each time I tell the tale, people approach me afterward, asking if I know where Luis is today. Did he go on to bigger and better things in middle school? Has he grown into a young man who looks back and points to folding tables in the cafeteria as his turning point and the beginning of his strength as a leader?

The truth is, I don't know. What I do know is, as much as the Custodian's Assistant story is about Luis, it's also quietly about Mr. Mario. Yes, I led the story by saying that

I'm always searching for youth in leadership roles. But at the same time that young Luis was practicing stewardship, he couldn't have made the choice to move into a leadership role without the invitation of Mr. Mario.

Luis was not the first student Mr. Mario noticed feeling alone in a crowded room. The cafetorium was not the only room Mr. Mario cleaned in the school building. Throughout the day and across the campus, the kindest school custodian I've ever met saw students who felt excluded and alone. Having experienced similar times in his own life, Mr. Mario felt empathy for the students. He sought to protect, build up, and empower them to see themselves as valuable, not invisible. He didn't see himself as just a custodian, only responsible for tidying up the school. He believed he could make a difference in the lives of the school's students and faculty. Anything he could do for them would outshine anything he did to clean and maintain the building. Quietly and daily he invested in others. He didn't require a fancy title, and he never received a shiny key to the city. What Mr. Mario did was responsibly manage, supervise, and protect what had been entrusted to his care. He was thoughtful, respectful, and trustworthy. First with himself, and then with others. Every day he practiced stewardship before leadership. So when the school launched a campus-wide initiative to develop leaders, it was no surprise they included Mr. Mario in the training process. When the time was right, he too invited students like Luis into a leadership role. By doing so, Mr. Mario elevated the vision, raised their standards, and built the confidence and capabilities, skills and character of the students he worked with every day.

Looking back, do you see the progression Mr. Mario invited Luis into? From membership through stewardship and

up into leadership. First, how important was it for Luis to belong to a group? In addition to his natural membership in the student body and his grade level, he jumped at the opportunity of chosen membership as the custodian's assistant. Now, he could have just done his "job" and been on his way back to class at the end of lunch each day. But no, he made more of the opportunity. The responsible management, supervision, and protection of what had been entrusted to Luis's care included the after-lunch conversion of the cafetorium and how he chose to invite other students into the group. Their interest in what he was doing, how he was doing it, and how willing he was to share the credit for quality outcomes earned him a leadership role. Luis wasn't in it for the rank or position. He thrived in the role, the responsibility of cleaning up the cafeteria, while lifting up his classmates at the same time. He practiced stewardship before leadership and that's exactly what first impressed us all. Being rewarded with the Jr. Key to the City is how people showed their appreciation for his leadership.

So, what are the factors that elevate people who practice stewardship up into the level of leadership? There are five qualifications for leadership:

1. You remain connected to and identify with your groups of membership.
2. You practice stewardship, even if you are the only one affected and nobody is watching.
3. You earn others' interest in what you are doing.
4. You are willing to share successes.
5. You believe sharing will influence others' experience in membership, improve their practice of stewardship,

and strengthen their ability to match and exceed you in leadership.

Pause for a minute and carefully consider factors 4 and 5. Willingness to share means you are choosing to release control of what others are also interested in doing. You may be the only one with the recipe to the secret sauce, but you are willing to share so others can fully experience membership, practice stewardship, and strengthen their ability to *match* and *exceed* you in leadership. This means factor 5 makes your leadership role temporary. Temporary because once others match and exceed you, they no longer need you to provide them leadership. They are either standing right beside you, have taken a step ahead of you, or are launching out on their own.

This is why it's so important that when you reach the level of leadership, you remain fully invested in your membership while always practicing stewardship. The best leaders maintain all three at once. The group knows who they are, they act responsibly, and from time to time, others show interest in how they see, think, and act different. Those who choose to share and believe that others can be even better than them repeat the cycle from the role of leadership.

Key Elements of Leadership

These five factors of leadership are a good start. But what else do people in leadership provide that will influence how others experience membership, practice stewardship, and strengthen their ability to match and exceed the abilities of leadership? For you to be the kind of leader our world needs, you'll have to provide people with four additional elements of leadership:

1. Compelling **Vision**
2. Specific **Direction**
3. Meaningful **Protection**
4. Timely **Succession**

Vision

Leadership provides a compelling **VISION** others can see. A compelling vision is a clear mental picture of a desirable future. Often just over the horizon or right around the corner, vision is seeing ahead in ways others have not yet. Visionary leadership is about seeing and creating a new reality that improves upon what already exists. Sometimes difficult for others to picture, a leader's vision must be more than romantic hopes and wishes. For others to see what you see, your vision must hold a level of value and specificity that compels people to believe the leader's vision not only needs to be accomplished but that it can be accomplished.

> *Vision is a clear mental picture of a desirable future.*

Direction

Leadership provides specific **DIRECTION** others can follow. Direction is the understandable course to take in pursuit of a vision. Getting from where we are now to where we want to be requires a leader to possess levels of knowledge and understanding, abilities, resources, processes, and accountability that convince others their direction can be trusted and followed. It's important to note that specific direction

does not mean micromanagement. Constant intervention and correction limit others' practice of stewardship and communicates a lack of trust in others' abilities.

> *Direction is the understandable course to take in pursuit of a vision.*

Protection

Leadership provides meaningful **PROTECTION** others can depend upon. Protection is the act of preventing someone or something from suffering harm or injury. Protection also includes defense when needed. Yet more effective than a leader who jumps into the fight is a leader whose direction avoids the fight altogether. Small course corrections along the way may go unnoticed by most people, yet leadership that keeps its eyes ahead and makes incremental adjustments to avoid potential conflicts is offering the kind of proactive protection people prefer over reactive defensive moves. This doesn't mean leadership is proven by a lack of hardship. On the contrary, difficulty and progress often walk hand in hand. For a leader's vision to become reality, they are guaranteed to face high hurdles, tough climbs, and hard decisions that will affect other people. Leaders who treat others with the same consideration they want to receive can be depended upon to protect others just as they would want to be protected.

> *Protection is the act of preventing someone or something from suffering harm or injury.*

Succession

Leadership provides timely **SUCCESSION** others can plan for. Succession is the planned passing on of value, one person after another. At the core of leadership is the belief that the next to hold the leadership role can meet and exceed your performances as a leader. The person who believes nobody else can lead as well as they can is delusional. They have been fooled by their own perception of power and a misunderstanding of the role of leadership. Leadership is a choice and leadership is temporary. In the short time allotted, good leaders are actively looking for stewardship in people who are responsibly managing, supervising, and protecting what has been entrusted to their care. As we discussed a few pages back, stewardship is a model for how those who can be trusted with little can be trusted with much more. And when it comes time for succession, stewardship reminds those who have been trusted with more that much will be expected of them. These are the people who get invited into leadership. They are the next generation of even better leaders. From small delegations to ultimately passing the torch, succession is empowering to both the giver and receiver. Empowering because when the transition goes well, vision can be expanded and new opportunities pursued. Where one leader saw just over the horizon, the next sees an even farther shore.

> *Succession is the planned passing on of value, one person after another.*

So what do you think about membership, stewardship, and leadership now? Will the principle of *practice stewardship*

before leadership challenge the way you see, think, and act different? Because *different* is what the next generation will need to do and be if you are to not simply repeat the two-layer leadership terms of your parents. Remember, if we want to achieve different outcomes, it's best to practice different methods. Yes, all generations need good people to fill important leadership roles. Nothing has changed there. What is different is that the three-layer model of membership, stewardship, and leadership sought by today's emerging generations is taking the place of the previous leaders-over-followers model.

CONSIDER THIS:

Marie Skłodowska Curie was a very unique leader who thought and acted different than her colleagues. A Polish-born French scientist, she became the first woman to win a Nobel Prize, for her research into radioactivity, and the first person to win a second Nobel Prize, for chemistry. She remains the only person to have won two Nobels in two different sciences.[6]

YOUR TURN:

1. List three people who you believe have been exceptional examples of leadership.

   * _____
   * _____
   * _____

2. Focusing on one of the people you listed above, what was the specific vision, direction, protection, and succession they provided to others?

- Vision: _____
- Direction: _____
- Protection: _____
- Succession: _____

3. Think of your friends and the other young people you know. Who do you believe possesses the greatest leadership potential? What brought you to think that about them?

_____

_____

_____

_____

4. What about you? How are you demonstrating the qualities of good leadership?

_____

_____

_____

_____

Challenge 3
TRANSFORM RAW TALENTS INTO VALUED STRENGTHS

Work to make the most of yourself.

Chapter 8

VIEW FROM 30,000 FEET

"We have been unintentionally misleading our youth for years by misrepresenting the capabilities of their talents and understating the value of their strengths. Teachers are guilty of it along with coaches, bosses, and especially parents."

Now if this statement leaves you a bit confused and asking for more information, you are feeling just as I did when the woman sitting beside me on the plane said it. A bit taken aback, I asked her for some clarification. What she said next she stated with such confidence that I was convinced she had given the same speech a hundred times before. And you know what? She had.

"Now don't get me wrong," she began. "They are innocent and unintentional errors. Like when an English teacher writes an encouraging note on a student's homework saying, 'You are a very talented writer.' Or when a coach travels across the country to recruit a 'talented' quarterback to lead his team."

As she continued, I reached down under the seat in front of me to get a notebook out of my carry-on bag.

She continued, "Senior partners in a legal firm pride themselves on only hiring the most talented attorneys. A proud parent posts pictures from their child's music recital with the caption 'We are so proud of our talented pianist.' As harmless as each of these sounds, they are all quite inaccurate. Each misattributes 'talent' as the reason for exceptional performance."

When I asked if she would mind my taking some notes while we talked, she emphatically replied, "Please do." At the same time, she handed me a pen. Printed on the side of the pen was the logo of a well-known university. Checking my watch, I noted that our scheduled landing at the Dallas/Fort Worth International Airport was still over an hour away, so I continued to ask the woman questions. Turns out she was a senior faculty member at the university whose logo was on the pen she had given me. That day she was traveling to deliver a talk at a conference for educators. That stirred my interest, and I asked about the topic of her upcoming speech.

"It's about the talent crisis we are facing in America. Truth is, we're really facing a *strengths* crisis," she said. "A crisis that begins with our misunderstanding of talent."

She went on to explain how her university receives thousands of applications each year from high school seniors, international students, and transfer students all anxious to be accepted to their "dream" university. Each student's application is reviewed, categorized, and carefully considered for possible acceptance. As she explained, this process had become increasingly difficult, as most applicants are what many people describe as very "talented." Their merits include high grade-point averages, outstanding performances

and awards, committed participation in clubs and sports, countless volunteer service hours, and shining recommendations from prestigious professionals.

Curious about how the university filtered through the glut of qualified applicants, I asked how they addressed the issue.

She explained that one of their breakthroughs in the application process was asking students to describe their strengths and weaknesses, and how each influences their purpose in life.

Wanting to learn more, I asked how students answered this great question.

"I'll tell you what they *should* say," the woman replied while tipping her head to one side.

Pen in hand, I drew a star on my notes page in anticipation of the importance of the insider perspective she was about to share.

"You can write this down if you want"—she smirked— "but I don't think you're going to forget it." She continued, "They should answer our questions about their strengths, weaknesses, and purpose in life with, 'I'd like to start with my weaknesses—they include the fact that I don't know my strengths or purpose in life.'"

A short pause allowed my mind to fully register what she said. Then she continued. "But instead, they almost always repeat what people have told them about their talents. They answer, 'I'm a *talented* leader, or a *talented* football quarterback, or a *talented* public speaker.' But the problem is, that's not what we asked them."

"So, how should they do it? How should they properly describe their strengths, weaknesses, and purpose?" I asked.

Leaning on the armrest, she looked at me, smiled, and said, "We would love to have them say something like . . .

'I do my best to minimize my weaknesses and maximize my strengths. My strengths include visionary leadership while serving three terms on student council.'

'My strengths include earning the position of starting quarterback and team captain.'

'My strengths include standing as valedictorian and delivering an inspirational speech that has been viewed over 100,000 times on YouTube.'"

She elaborated. "We're really not too concerned about the specifics of their weaknesses. As long as they recognize they have them and are finding ways to work with, around, or reduce them. Mainly we are interested in learning if they know of their strengths, what strengths they want to develop, and how their strengths empower them with purpose in life. After all, that is the job of our university: to help students build, share, and multiply the value of their strengths."

Our conversation continued until the flight landed. We discussed the best practices of professional educators, the responsibilities of parents, and what the future might hold for your generation. In the end, we agreed the talent crisis we are facing today needs to be aggressively addressed. We concluded that a good starting point is to work on correcting many young people's misperception that they are going to make it in life on the impulses of their raw talents rather than the recognized value of their developed strengths.

We both agreed that talents are good, but since strengths are transformed talents, strengths are more valuable than talents.

So how do we help your generation move beyond your talents? Putting first things first, we need to correct our mis-

understanding of the difference between talents and strengths. Everyone has talent. Literally everyone. We are all born with natural tendencies or abilities that can be positively applied. Unfortunately, not everyone has strengths.

Oops, did that puncture the fragile shell we use to shield ourselves from feelings of inadequacy? It did, didn't it. Sorry, not sorry. The truth is, not everyone has strengths because many people leave their talents undeveloped. Maybe this is the fault of generations that came before you. In our attempt to not offend you, we deceived an entire generation with the lie that you are good at everything. Trophies for everyone! At the same time, we have failed a generation by not being honest with you about how on talent alone, you lack what it takes to be competitive. To be truly competitive requires developing actual strength.

Strength is the ability to make a positive contribution greater than what is expected in return.

This means people who have transformed their talents into strengths hold an advantage over those who haven't. For instance, the best coaches don't simply recruit talented athletes. Winning coaches recruit players with certain valued strengths who contribute what the team needs to win both in and out of competition. Likewise, the very best companies don't just hire talented people. They hire for specific strengths that will give their company an edge in the marketplace. The finest orchestras don't just put out a call for talented musicians. They seek premier artists who have mastered an instrument, can follow a principal conductor, and will contribute to the orchestra's overall performance.

Please don't misunderstand me here. I absolutely do believe talent is a critical component of quality performance.

But on talent alone, your performance is seldom consistent, rarely exceptional, and holds little lasting value to others. Without careful and consistent honing, most talents are best described as crude, unrefined, or raw. For raw talent to be transformed into a consistent, exceptional, and valuable strength, it must be refined and paired to function as one of four interdependent values.

In addition to identifying their raw **talents**, top performers pursue quality **training**, master the **timing** of practice and patience, and carefully steward the **treasures** of their life. The resulting outcome of talent, training, timing, and treasures is **valued strength**. It's for valued strength, not raw talent, that a top ballplayer gets drafted, a new employee gets hired, and a master musician is selected to sit first chair. To put it another way: Talent will get you recognized. Strength will make you renowned.

CONSIDER THIS:

The "participation trophy" may not be as new of a concept as we all think. Printed in the February 8, 1922, edition of the *Evening Independent* of Massillon, Ohio, a headline reads "Many Trophies for Tossers in State Tournament." The column begins with, "Trophies galore will be offered for the second annual Ohio State invitation high school basketball tournament." The piece goes on to state, "Members of the victorious outfits will be given individual trophies. A participation trophy also will be given to each athlete playing in the series."[1]

YOUR TURN:

1. What are your thoughts on the trend of giving everyone who participates even recognition? "Trophies for everyone!"

   • Benefits _____

   • Problems _____

2. In what areas of your life have you been told you are very talented?

   _____

   _____

   _____

   _____

3. If you were to one day become a top performer, what could you see yourself doing? What commitments might be required of you to transform your raw talents into valued strengths? List a few.

- _____
- _____
- _____
- _____

Chapter 9

TALENT

VALUE I

Talent
Naturally recurring patterns of thought, feeling, or behavior.

Strength

One of the world's most respected research and performance consulting groups is the Gallup Company. Founded in 1935, Gallup specializes in helping leaders and organizations solve their most pressing problems. One of Gallup's specialties is

assisting people in maximizing their potential at work and elsewhere. To better guide their clients around the world, Gallup worked diligently to clarify and define talent. What they concluded to be the uniqueness found within every human being is what they attribute as talent. This means the innate abilities you possess to perform well, consistently, likely from a young age, stem from your talents.

Throughout my years of working in character and leadership development, I have found Gallup's definition of talent to be one of the best. I believe you will too, and here's why. Gallup's definition of talent is precise and easy to remember.

Your naturally recurring patterns of thought, feeling, or behavior. [1]

As simple as it may appear to define talent, it can be a bit more difficult to identify what a person's talents are. For instance, take a minute to consider how aware you are of your talents. Go ahead, set a timer on your phone for sixty seconds and think about what naturally recurring patterns of thought, feeling, or behavior make you uniquely you. Ready, set, go.

60 - - - - - - - - - - - - - - - - - - 30 - - - - - - - - - - - - - - - - - - 0

Okay, time's up. Did you stay focused for the full sixty seconds? If, after a minute of introspection, you found yourself thinking this is tough, you're both right and not alone. Most people find it really hard to describe themselves as "talented." "Sure, I can see talents in other people," I hear them say. "But when it comes to seeing the talents within myself, I'm much better at recognizing my weaknesses."

True, knowing your weaknesses is an important aspect of keeping your life real. The problem is, many people aren't aware of or don't use the opposite positive forces in their life to make their life better. These positive forces are your *strengths*. Not to turn this into a physics lesson, but to forget how *for every action, there is an equal and opposite reaction* only adds force to your weaknesses. Instead, acting on your strengths helps take power away from your weaknesses and increases your successes. This takes some organization and coordination of your greatest potential, and it all starts with you seeing yourself as talented.

To help you start your talent search, try looking at yourself through a different set of lenses. Most people are quick to circle back around to focus on their weaknesses or what they do poorly. Instead, you are going to look for the things you already do well. For now, try not to be really specific—like how good you are in a particular sport, solving difficult math equations, sketching faces, or performing your job. Spoiler alert: these are not talents.

Start by looking for themes in how you do life. Replace *how good you are in a sport* with *are you considered a competitive person?* Competitiveness is a talent. Or how about replacing *solving difficult math equations* with *are you driven by being exact or precise?* Being precise is a talent not all people possess. In place of *sketching faces*, are you artistic? Being artistic is a unique talent. *How well you perform your job* is not your talent either. Instead, your talents influence how well you perform your work.

Try to see yourself as others see you. How would your friends describe the way they've seen you thinking, feeling, and behaving? How far back have they seen these traits in you? Might they say you have always been a curious person?

Might they describe you as persistent? Perhaps you are quick to display empathy or compassion. Would others see you as a visionary or unusually persuasive? Maybe you are extremely thoughtful or naturally physically coordinated. Maybe you have always had an eye for beauty or an ear for music. People might say you were "born to" help others, build things, perform, or lead. Maybe you are seen as observant, articulate, or accurate. Such descriptions could be shining a light on your naturally recurring patterns of thought, feeling, or behavior that, when positively applied, can be transformed from raw talents into valued strengths.

Give it another try. This time allow yourself more than a minute to think about the naturally recurring patterns of thought, feeling, or behavior—your *raw talents*—that make you unique. On the lines below, write down what you would consider to be your natural talents.

1. _____

2. _____

3. _____

4. _____

5. _____

6. _____

7. _____

8. _____

9. _____

10. _____

By identifying your raw talents, you have taken the first step in the empowering process of transforming them into valued strengths. Like any solid structure, the foundation matters. Think of your *raw talents* as a strong base to build your *valued strengths* upon. Without the foundation, you can't build much. With a solid base, what you build from here is up to you.

Perhaps your talent of curiosity and always asking why will build into a career as a forensic scientist, investigative journalist, or online reputation manager. Maybe your keen hand-eye coordination could develop from a natural physical talent into a career as a surgeon, an airline pilot, or a tower crane operator. Maybe you are that person who is always able to defend yourself and others with a very persuasive argument. You may not always be right, but you are never wrong. That sounds like you might make a great defense attorney, environmental activist, or politician one day. Each depends on what combination of raw talents you choose to invest in as you build your valued strengths.

CONSIDER THIS:

Considered the first televised talent show, the *Original Amateur Hour* aired on television between 1948 and 1970. Contestants in early episodes competed for audience votes cast by postcard or telephone. Winners received a trophy and "scholarship" check.

1. Who are the most talented people your age that you know? Remember our definition of talent: "naturally recurring patterns of thought, feeling, or behavior."

Name: Talent:

1. _____   _____

2. _____   _____

3. _____   _____

4. _____   _____

5. _____   _____

2. What about you? What are some of your raw talents?

1. _____

2. _____

3. _____

4. _____

5. _____

Chapter 10

TRAINING

VALUE 2

Talent
Naturally recurring patterns of thought, feeling, or behavior.

Training
Process in which one is taught the skills needed to perform a task.

Strength

When we stop for a moment and think about the concept of *raw talents* as the starting point of outstanding performance, we see that everybody possesses at least a few talents. In fact,

I've never met a person without talent. At the same time, I have talked with countless people who have no idea what to do with their talents. Maybe that is because from a very young age we considered "talent" and "professional" to be one and the same. Yet we are establishing the fact that they are not. Sure, raw talent will get you recognized. But you will never go pro on talent alone. Your talents need training: the process in which you are taught the skills needed to perform a task. For your *raw talents* to begin their transformation into *valued strengths*, you will need to build your skills through specific *training*.

Skills are the mechanics that enable a person to perform consistently well. What is unique about skills is how they

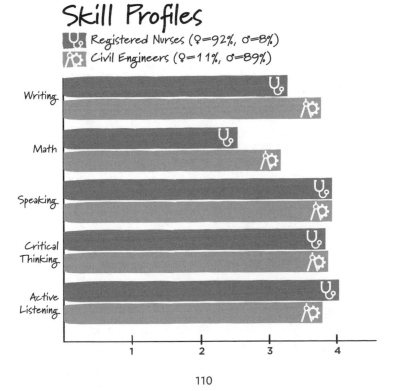

Skill Profiles
♀ Registered Nurses (♀=92%, ♂=8%)
♂ Civil Engineers (♀=11%, ♂=89%)

are fundamentally inclusive. Despite what some members of older generations may think, there are no gender-specific skillsets. This means there is no such thing as a "man's job" or "women's work." Skills are not masculine or feminine. So, neither are the *valued strengths* they build into. For instance, consider the skill profiles of registered nurses and civil engineers, meeting planners and construction managers, personal and home care aides and firefighters.[1]

Traditionally, registered nurses, meeting and convention planners, and personal and home care aides have been female-dominated occupations. Civil engineers, construction managers, and firefighters tended to be male-dominated workforces.

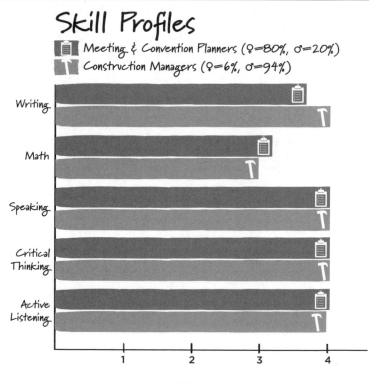

Skill Profiles

Meeting & Convention Planners (♀=80%, ♂=20%)
Construction Managers (♀=6%, ♂=94%)

Writing
Math
Speaking
Critical Thinking
Active Listening

1   2   3   4

But why? As these profiles demonstrate, the skills required to fulfill traditionally gender-specific roles have nothing to do with gender. True, some traditionally male-dominated roles demand physical strength. Yet it's also important to recognize there are no careers that hold standard strength requirements sufficient enough to exclude by gender. So the differences between the physical requirements of a traditionally male vs. female role are not what generations before yours once thought. What was once believed to be *different genders, different skills* is now *different genders, same skills*.

Breaking from the traditions of past generations, your generation is far more open to skipping gender stereotypes

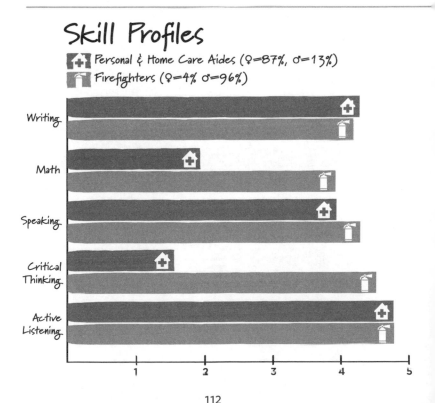

Skill Profiles

- Personal & Home Care Aides (♀=87%, ♂=13%)
- Firefighters (♀=4% ♂=96%)

to pursue training in skills you believe will be most personally and professionally fulfilling. Thank goodness! Many Boomers and Gen Xers consider this to be "nontraditional" career training because workforce gender equity is a new normal for many of them. I'm willing to bet your generation will simply call it career training.

FIND

I can almost hear you thinking, *Yes, I agree. No more sexism in any form of training. But now what? How do I find what training will best develop my talents?* Just as the themes

Strength Requirements
Male–vs.Female–Dominated Occupations

Legend:
- ♂ Male–dominated
- ♀ Female–dominated

Categories: Trunk Strength, Dynamic Strength, Explosive Strength, Static Strength, Stamina

of your talents can be identified by reflecting on the patterns in your life, so can the areas of your potential training. To help you **FIND** these areas of training, consider the following.

Fulfilling—Doing these things gives you great satisfaction.

Inspiring—You can't wait to do these things again.

Natural—It's pretty easy for you to do these things.

Design—It's like you were made to do these things.

What are those "things"? Really think about yourself for a minute. Again, you may need to look at yourself as your closest friend or a supportive family member sees you. How would the people closest to you, and most encouraging of you, describe what makes you feel most Fulfilled, Inspired, Natural, and in your Design? How far back have they seen you doing these things?

On the lines below, take some notes to capture your thoughts and help clarify what you are thinking. Consider this a first step in your talent development. By filling in the FIND lines, you should begin to see a pattern, or patterns, in your answers. That pattern will help you identify the specific skills training needed to begin building and transforming your *raw talents* into *valued strengths*.

Fulfilling—Doing these things gives you great satisfaction.

1. _____

2. _____

3. _____

4. _____

5. _____

Inspiring—You can't wait to do these things again.

1. _____

2. _____

3. _____

4. _____

5. _____

Natural—It's pretty easy for you to do these things.

1. _____

2. _____

3. _____

4. _____

5. _____

Design—It's like you were made to do these things.

1. _____

2. _____

3. _____

4. _____

5. _____

Need some examples of FIND?

The Athlete

Everyone knows that Megan, who is never able to sit still for long, is most satisfied when she is physically active. Inspired by the drive to compete and thrill of sport, she accepts an invitation to attend a weeklong soccer camp. There, coaches introduce players to dribbling, passing, and striking a soccer ball. The fundamentals come quickly to Megan, and it's not long before she gains the nickname "Skills." Her favorite part of soccer camp is the daily scrimmages. It was like she was made to play a strategic position on offense. To Megan, she feels at her very best outmaneuvering and outrunning defenders on her way downfield to score another goal.

Talents: physical coordination, competitiveness, determination, strategy

Fulfilling: physical activity
Inspiring: competition
Natural: footwork and ball skills
Design: offensive striker

Training: school or club soccer team

The Musician

From an early age, Reed always seems to be humming or singing along to his favorite songs. He often converts the living room in his parents' house into an elaborate concert stage. There he performs his favorite cover songs and original lyrics before adoring fans, including family, friends, and his pet dog. In elementary school, his pitch-perfect voice can be heard loud and clear over the crowd of children "singing" in the seasonal chorus concerts. Seeing how much he enjoys music, Reed's

mom enrolls him in music lessons. After a couple months of piano, Reed's teacher suggests he switch over to working with a voice coach. As much as he was progressing on the piano, it's obvious his first love is singing. When he plays the piano, he simply plays. When he sings, he performs!

Talents: vocal tone, creativity, entertainment, passion

Fulfilling: vocal melody
Inspiring: performing
Natural: tone, pitch, range
Design: singing

Training: voice lessons

The Mechanic

Always thinking and tinkering, Emma really likes both deconstructing and building stuff. She asked her parents so often if she could take things apart to see how they worked that her dad gave her a 250-piece professional tool set for her thirteenth birthday. He figured she's going to do it anyway, so she might as well have the tools to do it right. In the garage is her workbench. Neatly organized, there is a place for everything, and everything is in its place. Small engines, bike parts, wires, and every broken appliance her family discarded in the last three years all have Emma's fingerprints on them. In her eyes, there is no fix-it project she isn't willing to take on. She feels just as comfortable with greasy, stained hands as she does with brightly painted nails.

Talents: curiosity, mechanically inclined, patience, coordination

Fulfilling: working with hands
Inspiring: repair and build
Natural: mechanical
Design: fix-it and invention

Training: technical school

Get Active

Training is all about learning skills, the mechanics needed to perform a task consistently well. This makes the *training* segment of transforming *raw talents* into *valued strengths* all about discovering new ways of doing something. New to you, that is.

At this step of the process, very little learning includes innovating. Instead, while the information or technique being introduced seems new to you, it has most likely been around for a minute already. Like when a culinary arts student learns new knife-handling skills, it's pretty safe to say chefs have been slicing and dicing that way for years. Or when a student is learning video game development and animation, they are most likely writing the same code as those who previously attended the class. The trick to making training more than the slow transfer of boring information from one person's head to another's is the difference between *passive learning* and *active learning*.

Passive learning is just that—relatively inactive. Class lectures that go on, and on, and on, book reading, and watching YouTube videos for hours are all forms of passive learning. With a wide world of information available about almost any topic, you're not much more than a page turn, series of online clicks, or streamed video away from passively learning

about anything you want. Without much effort, the information of how to do something becomes your knowledge. As good as this all sounds, it's not as good as it gets.

Where passive learning creates knowledge, active learning creates skills. Training is all about learning skills and performing tasks. Training moves knowledge to the next level when active learning gets more than just your mind moving. Hands-on activities, interaction, experimentation, role-play, and evaluations that include a second chance at getting it right all lead to higher levels of success and personal growth.[2]

So where passive learning is like memorizing the recipe of your favorite sweet treat, active learning is getting in the kitchen and preparing the double chocolate chip macadamia nut cookies—just the way you like them.

Rarely does training by active learning happen independently. By independently, I mean working alone, all by yourself. Training by active learning requires interaction with other people and groups. By working with others, the training process becomes interdependent. Sure, I'm pretty good on my own (independent), but together we are so much better (interdependent). Group discussions, team projects, and crowd support are all powerful forms of active learning that make training far more real-world relevant while fulfilling our desire to belong to a meaningful group.

Of course, your best teachers, coaches, and mentors know all about the advantage active learning has over passive learning. Their hands-on, interactive instruction style takes active learning a step further by encouraging you to find ways to practice and apply your new knowledge. They know practice helps you determine what works and gives you an opportunity to do it again, as often as possible. The opportunity to practice also reveals what mistakes you made and gives you

another chance to not repeat them. When you meet adults who set you up for success with this kind of learning, please let them know they are doing something right. They know the applied knowledge, gained experience, increased proficiency, and expertise you are gaining are exactly what your generation needs to become the kind of innovators and creators who will change things. They also know the best version of you isn't developed in a one-and-done lesson. It takes time.

CONSIDER THIS:

Only four out of ten students who attend college complete their degree in under six years.[3]

YOUR TURN:

1. Consider the talents you listed at the end of chapter 9. What specific training might you FIND valuable as you begin to transform your raw talents into valued strengths?

Talent #1: _____

Fulfilling—Doing these things gives you great satisfaction.

1. _____

2. _____

3. _____

4. _____

5. _____

Inspiring—You can't wait to do these things again.

1. _____
2. _____
3. _____
4. _____
5. _____

Natural—It's pretty easy for you to do these things.

1. _____
2. _____
3. _____
4. _____
5. _____

Design—It's like you were made to do these things.

1. _____
2. _____
3. _____
4. _____
5. _____

Talent #2: _____

Fulfilling—Doing these things gives you great satisfaction.

1. _____
2. _____
3. _____
4. _____
5. _____

Inspiring—You can't wait to do these things again.

1. _____
2. _____
3. _____
4. _____
5. _____

Natural—It's pretty easy for you to do these things.

1. _____
2. _____
3. _____
4. _____
5. _____

Design—It's like you were made to do these things.

1. _____
2. _____
3. _____
4. _____
5. _____

Talent #3: _____

Fulfilling—Doing these things gives you great satisfaction.

1. _____
2. _____
3. _____
4. _____
5. _____

Inspiring—You can't wait to do these things again.

1. _____

2. _____

3. _____

4. _____

5. _____

Natural—It's pretty easy for you to do these things.

1. _____

2. _____

3. _____

4. _____

5. _____

Design—It's like you were made to do these things.

1. _____

2. _____

3. _____

4. _____

5. _____

2. What opportunity or access do you have to active learning (classes, clubs, courses, training, mentoring)? Consider avenues of active learning that match your FIND training:

1. _____

2. _____

3. _____

4. _____

5. _____

TIMING

VALUE 3

Talent
Naturally recurring patterns of thought, feeling, or behavior.

Training
Process in which one is taught the skills needed to perform a task.

Strength

Timing
Commitment to practice and patience.

No one knows who first posted the saying "Timing is everything." It was probably Captain Obvious. Important to comedy, love, introductions, apologies, and long road-trip bathroom breaks, we have all experienced the dramatic differences between good and bad timing, missed or perfect timing. Basically, timing is the particular point when something happens. Again, thank you, Captain Obvious. Still, there is another characteristic of timing that makes it so important in the construction of your strengths. Timing is also the careful balance of **choices**, **judgment**, and **control** of when something should or shouldn't be done. These factors are not random, and you can influence them through a commitment to practice and patience. The opportunities you develop, the quality of the decisions you make, and the mindsets and skillsets you master all require the kind of practice and patience only good timing allows.

The Power of Practice

It's just so easy to say. We grew up hearing coaches shout it, music teachers share it, and math tutors repeat the same statement over and over again. Go ahead and say it with me now.

Practice makes _____.

Did you complete the sentence with "perfect"? If so, oops. Sorry, but at no point in time has practice produced an actually perfect performance. This may feel like a slap in the face to those who also recall the false claim "Perfect practice produces perfect performance." Despite the catchy flow of words starting with the letter *P*, "perfect" still isn't possible.

By definition, *perfect* is determined by "having all the required or desirable elements, qualities, or characteristics;

as good as it is possible to be."[1] "As good as it is possible to be" sounds rather absolute, doesn't it? Sure, you can say you watched a perfect sunset last night or your favorite jeans fit you perfectly, but that's not what we're talking about here. The truth is, we rarely witness people perform in a way that fits the description of "as good as it is possible to be."

Instead, we regularly experience people performing in ways that have gotten better than what we previously believed to be "as good as it is possible to be." This mean that what was previously thought to be a perfect performance really wasn't. To be clear, whatever that person did was probably exceptional. Amazing, in fact. But if it really were perfect, would there be room for improvement? Technically, no. And it's important to understand why not. Stick with me, I'll show you why this distinction is so important.

With another common saying we acknowledge that this side of paradise, perfect is out of reach. Seeking grace for failing to meet expectations, we're quick to defend ourselves by saying, "Give me a break. After all, nobody is perfect." And when we want another chance, we might say something like, "With some practice I'll do better next time." Good. Now we're talking.

The truth is, practice does not make perfect. Instead, practice reveals three rules that within **timing** set your **talents** and **training** up to become your **strengths**.

PRACTICE RULE #1

Practice does not make perfect.
Practice makes better.

The "perfect" score of 10.0 for a single routine in artistic gymnastics was once considered an unobtainable Olympic

dream. That is, until Romanian gymnast Nadia Comăneci scored a perfect 10.0 in the 1976 Montreal Olympic Games.

As the fourteen-year-old Nadia stood confused by the scoreboard that read 1.0 (scoreboards weren't even built to register anything greater than 9.99), little did she know the perfect score of 10.0 would be awarded to her six more times in those legendary Olympic Games. At the conclusion of the 1976 Games, the petite teen returned home to Romania a national hero, wearing three gold medals, one silver, and one bronze. But that's not all. Four years later, Nadia Comăneci returned to Olympic stardom when she competed in the 1980 Summer Olympics in Moscow. She once again wowed the world by earning two additional perfect 10.0 scores, two new gold medals, and two silver medals.

So how did she do it? If perfect isn't possible, how did the little girl, whose mother described her as "a child who was so full of energy and active that she was difficult to manage,"[2] earn a total of nine perfect scores of 10.0 in Olympic competition? Two of which were in the same event, in back-to-back Olympics! Don't Nadia's performances prove perfect is possible? The answer comes from Nadia herself.

> People ask me, what is the definition of perfection? I say, there is none. There is no definition of perfection. At some particular time, when I was fourteen years old, I'd done something people didn't expect. I think it's a ladder you climb in life and I got there first.[3]

The young Queen of the Beam got there first. In the eyes of her 1976 and 1980 Olympic judges, Nadia's performances were considered *as good as it has ever been*, not *as good as it is possible to be*. This may sound like a subtle difference—"*it*

has ever been" vs. *"it is possible to be."* But this slight variation of thinking makes all the difference.

Between her 1976 Olympic performance and the 1980
games, Nadia practiced and practiced and practiced some
more. And she got better. This made her 1980 perfect 10.0
performance even better than her previous 1976 perfect 10.0
performance. She earned a new 10.0 by performing better
than *it has ever been*, thus demonstrating Practice Rule #1,
Practice does not make perfect. Practice makes better.

PRACTICE RULE #2

Practice makes possible.

Do you know how many young people I've interviewed over
the years who, when asked about their hopes, dreams, and
future plans, reply with one of the three following occupations? *I want to become a professional athlete . . . a famous
singer/musician . . . a millionaire YouTuber.* The answer is
thousands. Literally thousands of members of your generation have given me the same three answers about what they
hope to do one day.

Maybe you are not surprised by their aspirations. After
all, who hasn't imagined themselves living large? Especially
at a young age. What I do find odd is how consistent they
are in answering my follow-up questions.

Q: "What position do you play on the team?"
A: "Oh, I'm not on a team. I hate it how our coaches
   only play their favorite players so I'm going to wait
   till college to play. Then I'm going to go pro in the
   draft."

Q: "What instrument do you play?"

A: "I'd like to be a singer. I love to watch [fill in current popular TV talent show here]. My friends all say they would totally vote for me."

Q: "Tell me about your YouTube channel."

A: "I don't have one. My parents won't let me. They don't believe me about how easy it is for gamers to make money on YouTube."

Each of the above is a typical, youthful response. The problem is, each lacks the same key component: practice. They are looking forward to grand outcomes without a commitment to repetitive rehearsal. Sure, they may think about it all the time, have studied up and know all about it, and even be able to technically explain the performance—but there's a huge difference between knowledge about doing something and actually being able to perform. One skill is passive and the other is active. Passive may gain you knowledge of the subject while active yields both knowledge and the experience needed to build skills.

The difference between knowing and doing is so obvious if you have ever sat beside an adult who becomes an armchair referee or couch coach while watching sports on TV. Convinced they know everything about the game, they yell commands through the screen at the players, referees, and professional coaching staff working the sideline. Even though they haven't been in a game since their junior varsity season, thirty-one years ago, they lecture you on how getting the team to the playoffs is still possible, if only they were leading the team. They "guarantee it!"

The same can be said about a soon-to-be teen driver who tells their parents not to worry because they'll for sure be the best driver on the road. Even without a single mile behind the wheel, they truly believe those countless hours of simulated high-speed driving games are the same as real road time. Armchair politicians, the HGTV-watching self-proclaimed real estate expert, and your cousin's legal advice may all sound good, but could they really walk-the-walk if required? Keep dreaming. The simple truth is, without practice, dreams do not become reality. Not practicing is the same as not possible. This is why Practice Rule #2 is so important. *Practice makes possible.*

The big question is, how much practice is it going to take to make possible? That depends. Are we talking about the kind of practice required to possibly hear "Congratulations on making the team," or the kind of practice required to make possible Nadia Comăneci's Olympic records?

There's this really good journalist named Malcolm Gladwell. He's got a great speaking voice, amazing writing style, and really cool hair. In his 2008 bestselling book *Outliers: The Story of Success*, Gladwell writes about a study scientists did on stardom at the elite Academy of Music in Berlin, Germany. In the study the scientists looked into which students at the elite academy became the best. It turns out the school's truly "star" performers practiced an average of 10,000 hours by the time they were twenty years old.[4] This 10,000-hour measure came to be what many believe is the magic number of practice hours required for mastery. It was even given the catchy title of the 10,000-Hour Rule. So popular is the 10,000-Hour Rule that it has become the time-measurable aspiration of people who want to one day reach the very top of professional-level success. Unfortu-

nately, there is nothing magical about 10,000 hours. The truth is, if you start off lacking talent, no amount of racking up practice hours will make a person the #1 star they want to be.

Malcolm Gladwell was asked by a reader, "What is the most common misunderstanding you encounter from people who have read *Outliers*?" Gladwell's response helped clear things up about the myth of the 10,000-Hour Rule.

> There is a lot of confusion about the 10,000 rule that I talk about in Outliers. It doesn't apply to sports. And practice isn't a SUFFICIENT condition for success. I could play chess for 100 years and I'll never be a grandmaster. The point is simply that natural ability requires a huge investment of time in order to be made manifest. Unfortunately, sometimes complex ideas get oversimplified in translation.[5]

Gladwell's statement reinforces what gym coaches, music teachers, and math tutors have known all along, yet rarely say to avoid being shot at by protective helicopter parents. One thing is certain—it's ineffective to use training to plug a talent gap. Natural ability is a must for top performers. Natural ability and time committed to practice make top performance possible. Athletes who practice end up playing in games, scoring points, and getting recruited. Musicians who practice get invited to play in performances, win competitions, and record albums. Gamers who practice get to win games, gain followers, and earn an income online. Simply put, practice makes possible.

So what happens when we stop practicing? Great question. The answer is, Practice Rule #3 kicks in.

PRACTICE RULE #3

Practice does not make permanent.

In an interview for CNN's *Human to Hero* series, the now-retired gymnast Nadia Comăneci commented on what we all know to be true about Practice Rule #3.

> I remember everything, all the routines. I can't do them anymore because I don't practice anymore.[6]

To get her 10.0 scores, Nadia Comăneci committed herself to Practice Rule #1—Practice makes better—by averaging six to seven hours of practice a day, for years. With practice, she got better, and Practice Rule #2—Practice makes possible—gave her the opportunity to compete before the entire world. Olympic stardom and the need to redesign scoreboards to display 10.0 followed. Then, as expected, when she spent less time in the gym, she began to experience Practice Rule #3—Practice does not make permanent.

Consider Rule #3 in your own life. Have you ever been asked to play a musical instrument you haven't picked up in a long time? Tried to recite lines from a class play you were in back in elementary school? Played a game, swung a hammer, or attempted to do something after not regularly repeating the practice lately? The results are not usually up to the quality you'd like to believe of your abilities, once upon a time.

The Importance of Patience

At about six years old, I remember standing at the end of the driveway waiting for the ice cream truck to turn down the street toward my grandparents' house. With the sound

of sweet summer joy still a full block away, I danced on the sidewalk with a dollar held like a baton in my little hand. I couldn't wait to hand it off in exchange for my favorite hot-day treat, a cherry-and-pineapple-swirled frozen Missile Pop.

My anxious anticipation was obvious, and I can imagine only made bearable by how cute Grandma said I looked when I stood on my tiptoes, straining to see farther down the street. My adorableness must have worn thin, because my grandmother put her hand on my shoulder and said, "Just wait. It will be here soon. Patience is a virtue."

I knew what *patience* meant, but not *virtue*. I hadn't learned about that one yet. Patience I understood well, as I'd played the kids' album *Music Machine* song "Patience (Herbert the Snail)" far too many times to count. I really liked the low voice of the slow snail as I sang along karaoke style as Herbert crooned about having patience, not being in a hurry, and how to avoid worry.

So yeah, patience I'd heard about. But virtue, that one was new to my six-year-old mind. Hoping her answer would speed up my frozen delivery, I asked my grandmother what *virtue* meant. She explained that virtue is a morally good quality in a person. "Like being a good boy," she explained. So I must have caused my kind grandma slight concern when I turned to her and whined, "Then why can't 'hurry up' be a virtue?" Still, she smiled and laughed one of her heartfelt chuckles. I liked hearing my grandma laugh. But in that moment, I liked seeing the ice cream truck rounding the corner even more.

Grandma was right. I just didn't know it at the time. The ability to wait for something without getting angry or upset is an extremely valuable quality. The virtue of patience works together with practice to improve both your mental

and physical abilities. The more often your mind and body rehearse good performance, the more you can add to the performance. The more good timing you add to your performance, the greater your strength.

The practice and patience of timing is what separates those with head knowledge from those with real experience. Where once-a-week guitar lessons will increase your knowledge of notes, chords, and strumming, that half hour of instruction is not enough to make playing guitar one of your strengths. As any true guitarist will tell you, practice and patience are required to master the instrument. After years of daily practice, the calluses on their fingers should serve as proof enough.

Timing also functions as a filter. Plenty of people want to be really great performers. I hear it regularly in the aspirations of your generation.

"I want to become an airline pilot."

"Someday I'll perform on a Broadway stage."

"Being a psychologist is what I see myself doing in the future."

Excellent! Each of the above are strengths and all require transforming raw talents into valued strengths. After receiving training specific to the learning and skills needed to perform tasks, the demands of practice and the virtue of patience are what make timing the filter that separates people who are just interested from people who are totally committed. I don't know about you, but I don't want to sit on a plane piloted by someone who merely read about flight, watch a Netflix show directed by someone simply interested

in acting, or attend therapy with a person who kind of likes helping people. Timing demands more than head knowledge. Timing is all about commitment. Timing's practice and patience produce the experience required to develop a strength.

CONSIDER THIS:

To stay competitive, professional video gamers practice up to seventeen hours a day.[7]

YOUR TURN:

1. Thoughtfully consider your upbringing. How did what was expected of you regarding practice and patience affect what you expect in your generation today?

   _____

   _____

   _____

   _____

2. What in your life do you believe would improve with practice?

   1. _____

   2. _____

   3. _____

3. On a scale of 1 to 10, how committed to regular practice are you?

1   2   3   4   5   6   7   8   9   10
low   *high*

4. On a scale of 1 to 10, how would others rate your patience level for improved performance through practice?

Patience with yourself:

1   2   3   4   5   6   7   8   9   10
low   *high*

Patience with others:

1   2   3   4   5   6   7   8   9   10
low   *high*

Chapter 12

TREASURE

VALUE 4

What do you value most in your life? Not necessarily the single thing that holds the greatest worth, but rather the gathering of treasure you guard closely. Individually, each piece of treasure can be appraised with varying degrees of accuracy. Whereas your bank account can be accounted for down to the exact cent, the closeness of your family may be best measured by emotions. The two are far from equal in comparison. The same applies to your reputation and the price placed on the opportunities that lie before you. All are valuable, none are equal, and each affords you freedom to enjoy your strengths. At the same time, squander any of them and you can be blocked from fully enjoying and living in your strengths.

Guarding the treasure of your relationships, reputation, finances, and opportunities is a form of personal stewardship. Remember stewardship? The responsible management, supervision, and protection of something entrusted to your care. There are few assets in life more important than the people closest to you (your relationships), the quality of your character (your reputation), the management of your money (your finances), and the access you have to advancement (your opportunities).

Relationships

It has been said that no person is truly wealthy until they have something money can't buy. This makes relationships one of our greatest treasures in life. Authentic relationships are priceless and can't be purchased with cash or any other form of hard currency. The only way to earn such a treasure is through the investment of mutual respect, trust, integrity, patience, kindness, love, and forgiveness. Family, partners,

friends, teammates, neighbors, teachers—they all hold the potential of great value. To help make these relationships invaluable, follow this simple truth: Treat others just as you would like to be treated. Treat them like treasure.

A friend once told me his most valuable relationships are with the people who know him best and like him anyway. Believe me, he's right. We've known each other since early high school. Over the years, I've come to know more about the guy than anyone, aside from his wife. And you know what? The more I get to know him, the more I like him. I think it's because he doesn't fake much of anything. So much so, he's equal parts honesty and stubbornness. This makes the man remarkably trustworthy. His yes means yes and his no means no. You can count on it.

People invest in things they can count on. Like any good investment, a treasured relationship increases in value over time. The longer and more you wisely invest in a good relationship, the greater the return on that investment becomes. In time, what started as something small increases into far more than you ever imagined.

The same is true for a mismanaged relationship. The longer it goes unattended, the less value the relationship holds. Likewise, one large miscalculation in the stewardship of the relationship can wipe it out in a single withdrawal.

Stewarding the treasure of relationships gains and helps you maintain access to your strengths. Equally, mismanaging the treasure of relationships can limit your ability to function in your strength. Businesses know it. Teams know it. Families know it. Friends know it. Lovers know it. Even the military knows it. The military? Absolutely.

The United States of America invests a great deal of money in the might of its military. One of the greatest assets

in America's military are the highly trained personnel of Special Operations. Because of the valued strength Special Ops provides the US military, they are given elite access to the latest and greatest in weaponry, intelligence, and tactical training. This makes them highly capable of operating in extreme environments, under extreme conditions.

One mission-critical asset Special Ops carefully protects is the value of their relationships. These elite military personnel trust and rely on each other so deeply they consider one another "family." So, too, the effectiveness of their operational strength relies on the stability of operators' actual families back home. Commanders know the value of family and invest regularly in events and trainings to better relationships between husbands and wives, parents and children, partners, dating couples, and extended family. Basically, the greatest fighting force in the world understands that when family relationships at home are strong, the Special Ops family is strongest.

The same goes for you and me. When the treasure of our relationships is stewarded well, we perform at our very best. How are you investing in family, friends, work, neighbors, and community relationships? How much respect, trust, integrity, patience, kindness, love, and forgiveness have built up in these relationships? What can you do to show others that you treasure your relationship with them and that, by working together, you are better?

My favorite example of a treasured relationship is one of those *I can't believe that just happened* stories. Not in a million years would I have expected to meet a total stranger that I had so much in common with. Sure, stranger things happen every day, but on this day, I couldn't have imagined a more random, or cooler, experience.

A TREASURED RELATIONSHIP

I really enjoy gearing up and getting out of town. Way out of town. Like into the wilderness for a hike or camping. The beauty of nature does my soul good, and I've found Northwest Montana to undoubtedly be one of the most beautiful natural landscapes in the United States. From clear valley rivers running strong with trout and salmon to jagged peaks capped white with snow year-round, the vast spaces between are rich with wildlife, timber, and a sense of confidence shared by people who enjoy what can only be understood as the Montana way of life.

One of Montana's great natural jewels is Flathead Lake, resting in the shadow of Glacier National Park. Flathead Lake is a must-add visit for any nature lover's bucket list and hence why I jumped at an invitation to deliver a keynote speech for an event hosted just a few miles south of the lake's pristine waters. Imagine my surprise when I learned the venue was located in the hometown of one of my all-time favorite people. In a single trip, I could visit Flathead Lake, speak with influencers, and poke around the childhood stomping grounds of my great-uncle Ernie.

Arriving a full day early, I planned to take in some Big Sky Country and sleuth around in search of the homestead my great-uncle Ernie and his sister, Vivian, my grandma, knew as children. It took some time, but I finally found the place. Referencing a faded black-and-white photo, I managed to frame up the mountain's peaks just right, and to my surprise, there in the valley stood the same small structure Uncle Ernie and Grandma called home some seventy-five years before. Now a yard tractor garden shed, the hand-hewn timbers looked just as they had when the young brother and sister had posed for a rare Depression-era picture. I stood looking back and forth at the photo, the structure, and at the photo again for about an hour before finally locking it in my memory and driving back to town.

Later that day, while "just looking" around a small shop, I came across a historical compiling of the vital records of the people of Lake County and Lower Sanders County, Montana. There in the pages of the *Senyelemen—"Gathering" of Sacred Records of the Sqelix (People)* 1910–1960, I read through the names of my family, two and three generations before.

The next morning, I stepped out onto a stage to deliver an inspirational back-to-school address before an audience of around two hundred educators. To open the talk, I decided to share what a great privilege it was to speak in the hometown of someone I so greatly admired. As I drew my next breath, an anonymous voice rose from the audience. "Nobody great came from around here," they interrupted.

A bit shocked, I paused. Perhaps the mystery voice had tossed out the statement in an attempt to get a heckler's laugh or maybe they actually believed what they said. Whatever the reason, I took the statement as a challenge and felt the responsibility to defend both my family's honor and the history of the small Montana town.

"I beg to differ with you, sir," I rebutted in his general direction. "One of the greatest men I knew lived here in Ronan, Montana. Yesterday I searched for and found his family's homestead. From humble beginnings as the son of a poor farmer, he went on to great accomplishments. As a teen, he enlisted in the Army and fought in World War II. As a young fighter pilot with eagle eyes, he commanded the air in his P-47 Thunderbolt. On the ground he fought to liberate Jewish prisoners from German concentration and death camps. After the war, he returned to the States, got married, started a family, became a schoolteacher, coached basketball, and coinvented the breakaway basketball rim. He was one of the most successful coaches in the history of Oregon State high school basketball and . . ." Now, it was my intention to continue my statement by saying, "and he was my uncle," but before I could finish my sentence, I was interrupted once again. A man in the second row stood up, pointed at me, and said

loud enough for all his colleagues to hear, "And his name is Ernie McKie and he was my hunting partner, basketball coach, and like a second father to me!"

Again shocked, I paused once more. For the next few minutes, the man shared about what a great relationship he'd had with my uncle Ernie. It was like he and I were the only two people in the auditorium. Of course we weren't. Two hundred people sat listening in on our conversation.

It turns out the man's father and my uncle had been boyhood friends, right there in Ronan. Both sons of homesteaders, the two grew up going to school together, playing, fishing, hunting, and farming the land south of Flathead Lake. The years saw the barefoot boys grow into young men, and though separated by a call to duty and the lives they chose after the war, their close relationship always brought the two back together at least once a year, during Montana's fall hunting season.

Still standing in row 2 and not seeming to care that our conversation was far from private, the man continued. His voice broke slightly as he explained how much it meant to him the year his father and Ernie included him in their annual hunt. And then, that next summer, his dad decided he was old enough to travel by train to Portland on his own to attend Coach McKie's basketball camp. And thus became the pattern. In the summer, Ernie trained him in basketball and, in the fall, deer and elk hunting.

Not too many years later, the man's father died. It was no surprise when Ernie returned to Montana for the funeral of his lifelong friend and fellow outdoorsman. Following the memorial service, the man's son and Ernie got to talking. "I'm going to miss hunting season and basketball camp with you," he told Ernie. Without hesitation, Ernie responded, "What are you talking about? We're still hunting together, and you have at least one more summer of basketball camp before you'll be good enough to play in college."

For as many seasons as Ernie's life allowed, the two hunted deer, talked basketball, and told stories about hunting deer and playing basketball. Like a second father, Ernie helped him through some of life's greatest transitions—like the loss of a father, the transformation between boyhood and manhood, choosing a college, and career decisions.

Ernie McKie died of cancer at only sixty-one years old. His memorial service was hosted in the same gym where he coached players into teams and teams into champions. West Linn High School's basketball gym can hold about a thousand fans. On the day of Ernie's memorial service, they maxed out the bleachers and court seating to beyond capacity. Gathering to celebrate his life were family, friends, students, old Army buddies, fellow coaches, former players, NBA stars, fishing friends, and a young hunting partner from Ronan, Montana, turned educator and coach.

Reputation

What is your reputation worth? This is the question my friend Mike Mooney asked me a few years back. Mike is a real pro when it comes to a person's reputation. Literally. He's a professional at shaping, protecting, and rebuilding reputations. His work with reputation management has formed him valuable relationships with the biggest and best companies in the auto, home improvement, household goods, banking, food and beverage, telecommunications industries, and the fast-paced world of motorsports.

The groups Mike works with are all very serious about their reputation management. So much so, they employ teams of people to carefully craft, monitor, and regulate their brands' images. And when it comes to helping them get their reputation right, they call on Mike.

It's cool that Mike gets to consult with big companies. It's even cooler that he has also dedicated himself to helping individuals—ordinary people like you and me—to be good stewards of our reputations. So when Mike asked me the very personal question, *what is your reputation worth?* he really got me thinking.

So much rides on the shoulders of your reputation. What this means is that for a young person like you to live in your strength, the treasure of your reputation needs to be stewarded as carefully as your talent, training, and timing.

A few years ago, a former student of mine told me a shocking story about something that happened at her parents' law firm. She explained that each year the firm offered two internships to college students interested in one day becoming an attorney. If the student and their internship are a good fit for the law firm, the law partners extend a scholarship offer to pay for law school once the student successfully gains their graduate degree. They continue to work at the firm while attending law school until they graduate and pass the bar exam. Upon passing the bar, they usually accept a full-time, well-paying job in the same law firm that helped them discover and develop their strength as a lawyer.

What a great opportunity! Her story almost made me wish I had known her father when I was considering career paths. Then she told me the shocking part of the story. That year, one prospective intern had really stood out from all the other applicants. Their college studies and activities were excellent, their references impressive, and they interviewed exceptionally well. With eyes set on practicing law and politics, the young ambitious college student seemed to be a sure thing for one of the two prized internships. That is, until the law firm ran a background check on their social

media posts. What they discovered did not speak well of the applicant's online reputation. Their posts regularly included lewd and rude language, partial nudity, and questionable reposts. Where their live interviews with the law firm had presented so honorably, the social media posts they chose to make public were building a "virtual" yet very actual reputation that was far from what the law firm wanted to be associated with.

Not surprisingly, the student was passed over for the internship, scholarship, in-school job, and full-time employment at the prestigious law firm. Total value, over $225,000. In a way, that was the price of their reputation.

To further emphasize the point, consider the people in recent years who landed themselves in headline news reports and social media memes alike due to bad decisions, pain inflicted, lies told, or crimes committed. From music producers to Hollywood executives. NFL Super Bowl winners to Tour de France champions. Teachers to politicians. Their reputation wrecked, and in some cases completely destroyed, most of the people you thought about have been suspended from performing the strength they worked years to master. Their talent, training, and timing remain intact. But their treasure has been tarnished by poor stewardship of their reputation.

The same goes for big business and small companies alike. Financial institutions, social media platforms, sports governing bodies, car companies, food distributors, and medical providers . . . just to name a few. The court of public opinion has tried and convicted many corporations whose reputations have crumbled under the pressure of profit over protecting the people who once trusted them.

So how about you? How about your generation? What are your reputations worth? A relationship? Financial scholarship?

A career? Switch gears with me here. Instead of considering what might be lost from a damaged reputation, consider what is gained by building a good reputation. Like a friend for life. The means to pay for an education. The career of your dreams. Each is the potential reward of a good reputation.

> Choose a good reputation over great riches;
>> being held in high esteem is better than silver or
>> gold. (Prov. 22:1 NLT)

Finances

People's views about money vary greatly. We can't seem to agree if money is the root of all evil or if money affords true freedom. Some say money can't buy happiness while others point to the fact that it takes money to buy tickets to Disneyland, and that's the happiest place on earth. Kidding aside, like it or not, money is part of almost every aspect of your life. This makes finances a treasure that must be stewarded carefully to gain and maintain the ability to afford (pun intended) to live in your strengths.

Finances. The management of amounts of good old-fashioned green dollars. You know, money. How much green you make, save, spend, and give away becomes your budget. If you live within your budget, all is good. Technically, this is called being "in the black." Spend more money than your budget allows, and you'll be in financial trouble. This is called being "in the red" financially. Caring for the treasure of your finances means keeping the green in your budget in the black.

So, what color is your budget? Do you even have a financial budget or just a feeling for what life costs and how much you spend to enjoy it? There are countless suggestions on

how much to spend and on what should take priority as you practice making and living on a personal budget. We're not going to dive into that pool of cash in this book. Instead, let's examine what will benefit you and your generation most when it comes to budgeting for a life that is a financial blessing rather than a financial burden.

1. **Know the numbers.** It's important to realistically understand both the cost of living and the income required to maintain a particular lifestyle. It's a really good plan to learn about budgeting before the practice of free spending becomes a habit that drives you into debt.

2. **Set goals.** Goal setting is not a complicated practice. The problem is, many people don't yet know how to properly see, set, and pursue their goals. *To assist you in effective goal setting we will discuss TIME of your life goals in Chapter 17.* In addition to earning and spending, it is important to set specific financial goals for saving, debt management, giving, and yes, even retirement.

   NOTE: One person's financial goals should not negatively impact others. For instance, if you don't want to be burdened with college debt, you should not guilt your parents into sacrificing their retirement savings to pay for school.

3. **Create a plan.** Those with a financial plan do so much better than those without. Specifically, those who plan long-term and who are willing to course correct as needed are more likely to stick with their goal. Good

financial planning includes taking steps that lead toward the goal and a realistic understanding of how long each step should take to accomplish.

4. **Measure progress.** Our brains like data. The proof is all around us. From easy-to-understand gauges on a car dashboard to instantly updated scoreboards in a sports arena. From watches that count our steps to apps that track social media likes. We are tuned in to knowing how things are going, right now. The same should be true about the status of your money. It's important that you interact with more than an occasional confusing bank statement. Rather, you need a compelling report that visually shows your current place and progress toward accomplishing specific financial goals. Thankfully, many banks have an app for that. Look for one that clearly reports if your financial goals are on track, at risk, or off course.

5. **Get accountable.** It's important to share financial goals with an accountability partner who can be trusted. A trusted accountability partner is someone who can say what needs to be said when it needs to be said. They are not someone who only says what you want to hear when you want to hear it. Meeting with an accountability partner regularly, on specific dates at a specific time, greatly increases your likelihood of accomplishing a financial goal.

6. **Celebrate accomplishments.** We all like to celebrate making it over the finish line. The same goes for rejoicing when a financial goal is met. The trick is to

avoid a financial setback by overspending in celebration. If the goal was to save money to buy a car, purchase the car. But if the goal was to pay off a credit card, it's only logical to not go on a spending spree in celebration of being debt free—temporarily.

One financial goal I suggest you make a high priority is to limit and eliminate your debt. With debt come the obvious restrictions tied to money owed. Like stress, pressure, and worry.

Less evident are the restrictions placed on your strengths. When your financial treasures have been spent or are owed to others, you become a version of a modern-day serf. Not surfer—they ride ocean waves. A serf feels crushed by the wave of debt. Serfs were peasants who lived under the bondage of legally binding debt. This meant they did not have the freedom to choose or change jobs, move to a new home, or enjoy personal and professional independence until the debt they owed someone else was paid in full. Technically, serfdom only lasted from the mid-1200s through the mid-1800s before being abolished. Yet many people today still live under the restrictions and pressure debt causes. And we're not just talking about people suffering under the conditions of extreme poverty in far-off countries. The burden of credit card debt, excessive loans, and uncontrolled spending have bound some of your neighbors, friends, and family to their current situation until their debts are paid. Like the serfs, they too can't afford to do anything until they are free from their legally binding debt bondage.

Debt can block your access to strengths. Treating your finances as a treasure means guarding your money carefully. Not to hoard, but to steward.

Opportunities

Most young people know the American poet Robert Frost from his famous poem "The Road Not Taken." There's a good chance you've seen the last few lines of the poem posted in an English class, printed on a motivational poster, or painted on a hall wall at school. The final words of Frost's poem are shared in hopes of inspiring young minds to carefully consider their options and not always follow the crowd.

> I shall be telling this with a sigh
> Somewhere ages and ages hence:
> Two roads diverged in a wood, and I—
> I took the one less traveled by,
> And that has made all the difference.[1]

Where the "two roads diverged in a wood" present two possible opportunities, only one choice can be made. Which road shall he walk? Frost chose the one less traveled. How that decision "made all the difference" has been the topic of debate by critics since the poem was first penned. We won't add to that argument today. Instead, let's allow the last stanza of the poem to get us thinking about how important it is to treasure the opportunities that present themselves in life.

Opportunity knocks every day. Sometimes it's a quiet tapping, while on other appearances it sounds more like desperate pounding begging for your attention. How you interact with the circumstances and the decisions you make related to opportunities comes from a place somewhere between ignorance and wisdom.

Wait, wait, wait. Before you allow yourself to get triggered by the word "ignorance," calmly consider that ignorance is one's lack of knowledge, information, and understanding. It

simply means "not knowing," whereas wisdom is having the knowledge and experience needed to make a good judgment call. Looking back on the process of how to transform raw talents into valued strengths, you'll remember that training is about gaining *knowledge* by learning the skills needed to perform a task. Timing gains you valuable *experience* through practice and patience. As the quality of your training and timing increases, so can your wisdom. If you use them both to make good decisions, you are acting wisely. If you simply don't know or lack the experience needed to make the most of an opportunity, well, good luck with the outcome.

Sure, everyone gets lucky from time to time. But do not confuse luck or chance with opportunity.

- You got *lucky* when your name was picked in an enrollment lottery to be accepted into a top-rated private school. You now have the opportunity to learn from some of the best educators in the area. You also have the opportunity to skip class and party.
- By *chance* you found a wallet containing credit cards, a driver's license, and $1,000 in cash. You now have the opportunity to find the owner of the wallet and return it, or the opportunity to keep it all for yourself.

Opportunity is a set of circumstances that make it possible to do something. Where luck and chance are random, the conditions that lead to an opportunity usually require hard work, can be planned for, and demand stewardship to keep.

- A film school student works for months on a short animation film, then she enters it into an arts festival

for the opportunity to be reviewed by judges responsible for issuing scholarships to the art institute she plans to attend next year.

- Though his SAT scores are good, by meeting with a tutor and taking the test a third time, he has the opportunity to score higher and bump up his college application profile.
- After submitting a job application online, you make time to visit the store for an opportunity to meet the manager in person to increase the likelihood of getting hired.

The key to making the most of every opportunity is to treasure your opportunities by using the wisdom gained from knowledge and experience to make choices you can be proud of. It doesn't matter if anyone else sees or knows what you choose. Integrity is doing the right thing, even when no one is watching. The path you take is up to you. But choose wisely—because it will make all the difference.

THE JOB OPPORTUNITY

You can learn a lot about someone by sitting and eating a meal in their dining room. I'm not talking about the fancy room in your house reserved for Thanksgiving dinner and special guests. Rather, the dining room of a restaurant. That's where the owner-operator of one Chick-fil-A franchise sits while conducting face-to-face interviews with potential employees.

"Interviewing people in the dining room during lunch or dinner hours lets me see how comfortable they are interacting with guests in a busy restaurant," he told me. "I can tell pretty quickly if they are

a good fit for our culture by the way they respond to kids, parents, construction workers, and businesspeople all mixed together. I can teach them all about chicken sandwiches, but it's just getting too difficult to teach them hospitality. So I look for people with people skills first, then restaurant skills.

"The easiest hire we ever made was decided before the interview even began. It was a stormy day with heavy wind and rain. The store manager and I scheduled the interview for noon, and the young woman who we were to meet arrived right on time. Except, by the time she made it from the parking lot to the dining room, she was a few minutes late and her hair was totally windblown and sopping wet. She politely asked to quickly straighten up in the restroom before starting the interview. My manager and I looked at each other, and with a knowing nod, we agreed. As the applicant stepped away from the table, the manager told her not to rush, we had already made our decision. She was hired."

Continuing, he explained their decision was made in the four minutes the young woman took to make it from her car to the building. Watching through the window, the owner and restaurant manager had seen her park, hop out of the car, and make a run for the front door in an attempt to get out of the storm's gusting wind and driving rain as quickly as possible. Just steps from the door, she noticed a mother back in the parking lot struggling to get her young children unbuckled, out of their SUV, loaded into a stroller, and headed into the restaurant. Stopping, she turned back to assist the woman and her children. Ignoring the wind and wet, she even patiently held open the restaurant door for the family so they could get into the building quicker.

"That's exactly the kind of team members we want," the restaurant owner said with enthusiasm. "She had every opportunity to just step inside and start her interview. Instead, she chose to set her own needs aside to help someone else. There's no on-the-job training for that!"

CONSIDER THIS:

Back in 2004 Americans reported, on average, they had about nine close friends.[2] With the mass acceptance of friends following friends on social media we might think this number has increased. When we do the math, it's debatable. Recent data now reports that Americans, on average, say they have sixteen*ish* "friends." This accounts for the three who are friends for life, five they really like and would hang out with one-on-one, and eight people who are liked but are not considered close enough to spend time with alone.[3]

YOUR TURN:

1. List a few members of older generations in your life with whom you want to gain or maintain a quality relationship.

   * _____
   * _____
   * _____
   * _____
   * _____

   What is the most important thing you can do that will show to each of them that you greatly value the relationship?

2. In the table below, write one word to describe the reputation of each of these people. On a scale of

1 (low value) to 5 (high value), how valuable is that reputation?

Name:	Reputation:	Value:
1. _____	_____	_____
2. _____	_____	_____
3. _____	_____	_____
4. _____	_____	_____
5. _____	_____	_____

3. Who can you talk to about learning good financial stewardship in your life?

_____

_____

_____

4. What is one opportunity in your life you already know you *wisely* took full advantage of?

_____

_____

_____

5. Looking back on the value you received by acting on that opportunity, what additional opportunities are you looking forward to making the most of?

_____

_____

_____

Chapter 13

STRENGTH

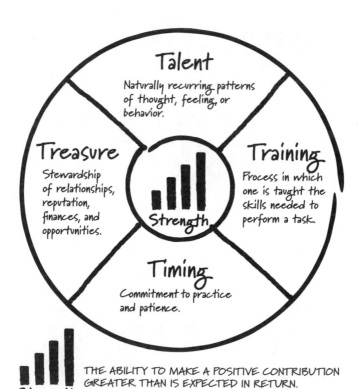

THE ABILITY TO MAKE A POSITIVE CONTRIBUTION
GREATER THAN IS EXPECTED IN RETURN.

We really like the concept of strength. Around the world, we admire strength in athletics, communications, business, relationships, and certainly in Wi-Fi signals. When we have access to strength, we're more focused and fulfilled. When we lack strength, frustration finds its foothold. Strength represents the best of what is available and often compensates for what is lacking. So shouldn't strength be a high priority for what we seek to develop within ourselves? The greatest performers understand this. They know how their talent, training, timing, and treasure all come together to allow them the ability to accomplish great feats.

Upgrading Strength

By defining strength as the ability to make a positive contribution greater than what is expected in return, we establish the difference between performing a task and contributing value. This distinction is what separates membership from stewardship and should be an unquestionable qualification of anyone in a leadership role. Contributing more than what is expected in return is what helps teams win games, groups make progress, performers wow audiences, and businesses become profitable.

Likewise, what upgrades a strength to a valued strength has a lot to do with supply and demand. If a person's specific strength is in high demand yet low supply, it will be valued more. When that same specific strength becomes common, it also becomes valued less. The strength a second-string college quarterback brings to the football team becomes far more valuable when the starting QB breaks his throwing hand. The strength of being an iron worker becomes a valued strength when certified robotic arc welding is added to a

résumé. The strength a soldier brings to the military becomes a valued strength when she earns her wings as a naval aviator.

Think back with me to the story I shared about the conversation I had with the university faculty member while flying cross-country at 30,000 feet. As you will recall, she was headed to a conference to present about the talent crisis we are facing in America. Remember how she said America is really facing a strengths crisis? I'd like to expand her statement to include the fact that we are facing a *valued* strengths crisis in America. In many ways, it's a crisis of our own making. Well, by generations older than you. Once upon a time, they believed that simply gaining a college degree presented graduates with a diploma, or all the "strength" they needed to go out into the world and get a good job and live the American dream.

The common path many members of Gen X and Boomers took included going to college as the ultimate plan for their future success. Some would argue that this is because the training a four-year education provided was more valuable than other options available at the time. For people like me who "adulted" in an era when a printed phone book was a necessary job-hunting tool, I will agree. But not so much these days. I'll challenge anyone to use the argument that a four-year degree is best on employers who can't find enough qualified applicants with valued strengths to fill their well-paying job openings that don't require a bachelor's degree. They'll say something about the value of a low-tuition education that lands career and tech grads in satisfying, high-paying jobs while so many college grads are in debt up to their eyeballs, unemployed, and moving back home.

Let's be perfectly honest. College isn't for everyone. It's time many adults stop stigmatizing those who choose not to go. Most of your parents and grandparents probably

remember high school "voc-ed" classes as options for kids who were more suited for blue-collar work after graduation. With or without a diploma, those who attended vocational training often stepped into lower-wage occupations while four-year-college-educated professionals earned higher salaries and a better shot at living the increasingly expensive middle-class lifestyle. Again, the cultural norm has shifted, and this is no longer the case for young people today. Jobs once considered "dirty jobs" have cleaned up and now demand a high degree of technical training that can be gained in a vocational school. Zap, Moore's Law strikes again.

The problem is, many adults are still sending out the message that pursuing a four-year college or university education is superior than shorter and less expensive training options. This has resulted in more than 600,000 skilled jobs remaining unfilled in the United States.[1] With an estimated 10 million new skilled workers needed in the next few years, companies are wondering who possesses the valued strengths they are looking to hire.[2]

Vocational, certified, associate's, bachelor's, master's, doctoral, or military ranks . . . it doesn't matter so long as the strength brought to the organization is valued and needed. So if you know how to transform raw talents into valued strengths, does that mean crisis averted? Yes and no. Yes to those who identify their talents, seek quality training, and commit themselves to the practice and patience timing requires and to the stewardship of their treasure. They will live in their strengths. Their valued strengths. For all else, no. Life is going to be a heavy lift. Sure, on talent alone they will get noticed. But it is because of their valued strengths that the best are recruited and hired, perform, and are promoted and celebrated.

From Raw Talents to Valued Strengths

The following are examples of the multiyear process people have gone through to transform their raw talents into valued strengths. Inspired by students I've mentored over the years, each is a testament of their commitment to finding and fulfilling their greatest potential.

The Athlete

Talents: Physical coordination, competitiveness, determination, strategy.

Training: School and club soccer teams. Personal trainer.

Timing: Two years club soccer, four years select team, four years high school team, four years college soccer, off-the-field training in nutrition and strength, and undergraduate degree in sports management.

Treasure: Family, friends, and teammate relationships. Only uplifting social media posts. Strong credit score and minimal debt. Attended sponsored clinics to meet professional players, coaches, and management.

Valued strength: Professional women's soccer, striker/ center forward.

The Musician

Talents: Vocal tone, creativity, entertainment, passion.

Training: Vocal lessons, school of the arts.

Timing: Six years private vocal lessons, four years guitar lessons, two hours daily guitar and singing practice, five high school musical productions, three community theater musical productions, ear training and development, vocal methods, acoustic training, and bachelor of arts in music.

Treasure: Communications with mother. Care for friends, castmates, and band member relationships. Quality online postings. Structured school loans, checking and savings plan. Trusted career manager.

Valued strength: In-studio music producer.

The Mechanic

Talents: Curiosity, mechanically inclined, patience, co-ordination.

Training: Vocational-technical school, vocational college, manufacturer certifications.

Timing: Three years high school vocational-technical school, two years vocational college, tech assistant job at local auto dealership, personal car builds, one year unpaid internship with Gibbs Racing, summer volunteer repair mechanic with Wheels4Hope, assistant supervisor with teen safety driving school.

Treasure: Close family relationships, manageable monthly income and expense budget, regular volunteer with NASCAR Foundation, in long-term mentorship.

Valued strength: Engine performance technician.

| CONSIDER THIS: |

Teams that focus on strengths every day have 12.5 percent greater productivity.[3]

YOUR TURN:

1. Have you seen one of your strengths increase to become a valued strength as demand increased? If so, what were the circumstances?

   _____

   _____

   _____

   _____

2. Have you experienced the opposite—one of your valued strengths decreased in value as demand decreased?

   _____

   _____

   _____

   _____

3. What pathways, both traditional and non-traditional, do you have access to, and how can you follow them to develop your strengths and increase your value?

   _____

   _____

   _____

   _____

Challenge 4
LIVE WITH PURPOSE

*Fulfill your vision, mission,
and goals in life.*

Chapter 14

ONE-OF-ONE

One of the most significant questions you can ask yourself is, what is my purpose in life? For those who know, meaning and contribution can be found in just about everything they do. For those who don't know, or don't believe in purpose, life can feel like a random set of circumstances that sometimes play to their benefit and sometimes don't. At least, that's what I've been told.

In my years of researching and in the personal interactions I've had with people who *live with purpose*, I've noted a significant difference between those who have purpose and those who do not. Those who know their purpose tend to be the contributors. Those who don't know why they exist, the consumers. As is the theme throughout this book, for you and your generation to *become the next great generation*, you will need to do and be even better than us. This will require you to look both within yourself and far beyond yourself to see and pursue the unique contribution you can make to the world.

To live with purpose begins with seeing the uniqueness of each life. We are all matchless. Despite the satire and jokes about Millennials and Generation Z being "fragile snowflakes," you really are each a one-of-one creation. We all are. The proof is coded right into your genes.

Did you know there are 8,324,608 possible combinations of your twenty-three chromosome pairs? To make matters about you even more exclusive, consider this amazing fact: the calculation of variant forms of human genes rounds out to approximately 70,368,744,177,664 total possible combinations. It's mind numbing to consider there are trillions of times more possible combinations of your genes than the total number of people who have ever lived. This means that nearly everyone, except identical twins, is a sole genetic creation. There really isn't anyone else on earth like you or me. So I guess it's both safe to state and a real compliment to say that members of your generation really are like snowflakes.

Now that we know how unique you are, take a good look far beyond yourself. Where in the world is your unique value needed? What can you offer? To find the answer, it's helpful to have a clear vision of where you are going, a mission that explains your *why*, and goals that will help get you there. Put simply, to *live with purpose* requires vision, mission, and goals.

Through my years of work and over two million miles of travel, I've had the opportunity to sit and talk with a number of remarkable people who live with purpose. Some were official interviews while conducting research, others simply casual conversations struck up in the moment. Hindsight being 20/20, I believe the barber-shop, lunch-line, long-plane-flight chats have proven to be some of my more prized exchanges. One such treasured talk was with a man who clearly knew

how his vision, mission, and goals empowered him to live with purpose. For the now-old man, it all started back when he was a teen, on the day he answered the call to help save the world.

THE WORLD WAR II SOLDIER

I was humbled to sit beside the WWII veteran who couldn't forget the hellish details of fighting the Nazis, yet now battled to recall the loving faces and names of his family. Over a slow meal and multiple cups of coffee, he relived decades-old war stories that deeply shaped his youth and adult life that followed. Toward the end of our meal, he turned to me and asked, "Do you know what that war did to me?"

"No sir," I replied.

"It taught me the importance of living with purpose." He smiled wide while looking me straight in the eyes. "I've lived a long time, and a long time ago, I decided the purpose of my life was to protect people. Three things gave me that purpose. Vision, mission, and goals. Do you know what's so important about vision, mission, and goals?" he asked. Without waiting for my reply, he took command of the conversation and began to teach me one of the most valuable and memorable life lessons I've learned. How to *live with purpose*.

As a teenager growing up in small-town America, he closely followed reports of battles fought between the Allies and Nazis. From gossip-talking in the corner store to dramatic newspaper stories of battles won and lost, the reports he followed eventually convinced the ambitious teen it was his time to contribute more to the war effort. Sure, conserving and rationing resources like fuel, metal, and tires was important. But he knew he could do more. In his imagination, he could clearly see himself standing up against enemies "hell-bent" on stripping nation after nation of freedom. He envisioned

himself fighting to regain what was taken, to secure what was deserved, and to defend what was right in the world. He wanted to fight for freedom.

It took some time and convincing, but eventually his mother agreed—he would enlist and join the fight. A few short weeks later and with strict instructions to write home often, he boarded a bus for boot camp. After that, who knows where. He didn't care so long as he was headed to the fight. The fight for freedom.

"Being a simple man, I like to pick one word to focus on. So my vision was for freedom. That is where I was going. Wherever freedom was threatened," he said with resolve.

VISION answers the question, WHERE?

While in basic training, his instructors drilled into the fresh recruit the mindset and skillset of a soldier. He learned how to look, move, think, and fight like a warrior. The training was difficult yet necessary to form boys into men. Men whose lives depended on each other and on whom the world could depend to accomplish their mission.

He recalled that one young recruit asked the drill instructor when he thought the war would be over. "When we march down the streets of Berlin! And do you know why?" the instructor barked. "Because when we are marching down the streets of Berlin, we will have won the war!"

Berlin was the word that stuck with him. Where his *vision* was to fight for "freedom," his *mission* became "Berlin." Not Paris, not Rome, but Berlin. Why Berlin? Because victory in the streets of Berlin would mean the war would end and the world would see freedom once again. Instead of seeing Berlin as a location, the city became a reason.

VISION answers the question, WHERE?
MISSION answers the question, WHY?

On June 6, 1944, all hell broke loose on the beaches of Normandy. With the vision of fighting for freedom clear in his mind and the mission of Berlin set in his heart, the scared soldier waded ashore on D-Day. By some miracle, he survived the largest and most deadly seaborne invasion in history. With the safety of home far behind, machine-gun fire all around, and his friends dying beside him, his goal that day was specific. To survive. To survive wading through bloodstained waters. To survive crossing the death-littered beach. To survive the worst day of his life. Yes, he secured the beach and, yes, he killed the enemy. That was what he was trained to do. But on that death-drenched day, and in many bloody battles to follow, he relied on his training as a soldier to accomplish the goal set in a single word—survive. The action he needed to take included whatever was required for him to survive getting from today through tomorrow.

> VISION answers the question, WHERE?
> MISSION answers the question, WHY?
> **GOALS answer the question, WHAT?**

"Because I did what it took to survive, I lived to march down the streets of Berlin, and see freedom restored to innocent people once again."

Is it difficult to think of a teenager finding their purpose in life through surviving the pains of war? It is to me. But this honored war veteran did. I'm thankful most of us won't be forced into such a horrific means of discovery. Still, as a teenage soldier, the now-old man learned one of the most important lessons of life—the value of living with purpose. He discovered *where* vision could take him, *why* mission matters, and *what* had to be done to accomplish his goals.

While still young, he learned that *where*, *why*, and *what* all work together to create a framework for how to *live with purpose*. Even after he battled his way through Europe, vision, mission, and goals continued to guide him. Upon his return home, he followed vision, mission, and goals to define his purpose in getting a good education. In building a successful business. In raising a family. And in growing his faith. In turn, he lived a long and meaningful life because he lived with purpose.

Unfortunately, far too many people live without such direction. They rise each morning, put two feet on the floor, and go about their day without believing they have any real or valued purpose in their life. From their perspective, little of what they do is memorable and even less is meaningful. Some describe the feeling like they are just simply existing.

The good news is, purpose exists for us all. Discovering it can be tricky, so try using the model of vision, mission, and goals to define your *where*, *why*, and *how* your life finds purpose.

CONSIDER THIS:

"While Millennials seek jobs that provide stability, convenience, and balance, Generation Z is more readily concerned with fueling their passions and taking pride in the work they do. For the first time, we see a generation prioritizing purpose in their work."[1]

YOUR TURN:

Your life is unique, yet also serves as an example for others. Complete the following sentence:

The purpose of my life is _____

_____

_____

_____

_____

Chapter 15

VISION DEFINES YOUR *WHERE*

Vision is a clear mental picture of a desirable future. Think of vision like standing on your tiptoes to see over the horizon or tilting your head while trying to look around a corner. True, you can't actually see over the horizon or around a corner with your eyes. But you can with your imagination. Vision requires you to use your imagination to picture a desirable future. Now before you say, this all sounds like hippy talk, stop and consider how much we already use vision when we hear people say,

> "When I graduate high school, I see myself going to State University."

> "I'm really looking forward to relaxing on a sandy beach on my next vacation."

> "Someday we'll start a family. I think we will make really good, loving parents."

"I can totally see myself being a teacher someday. I
know it doesn't pay well, but I believe teaching kids
would be really fulfilling."

Are not each of these statements clear mental pictures
of desirable futures? See, vision is already part of how we
do life. We regularly imagine or see ourselves in the future.
The question is, how meaningful and purposeful is your vision
for the future?

How would you answer these questions: What do you see
yourself *doing* in one year? How about in three years? Or
five? What about ten years from today? How far out into the
future does your vision extend? Give it a try.

What do you see yourself doing?

One year from today I see myself doing

_____

Three years from today I see myself doing

_____

Five years from today I see myself doing

_____

Ten years from today I see myself doing

_____

Now try a slightly different variation of the same question: Who do you see yourself *being* in one year? See the
difference? It's subtle yet significant. Doing vs. being. First,

you answered questions about your actions. That's doing. Now, what is your vision for your character? That's being.

Who do you see yourself being?

One year from today I see myself being

_____

Three years from today I see myself being

_____

Five years from today I see myself being

_____

Ten years from today I see myself being

_____

Look at your answers, how you filled in the blanks about both doing and being. Now consider these questions:

- Are they related to each other in any way?_____

  _____

  _____

- Is what you want to do and who you want to be complementary to each other? If so, move in that direction.

  _____

  _____

  _____

- Do you see any conflicts? If so, pause and determine why. _____

_____

_____

Correcting any potential conflicts now will save you a lot of time and help keep you out of trouble in the future.

CONSIDER THIS:

Skills make a person valuable.
Character makes a person invaluable.

Chapter 16

MISSION DEFINES YOUR *WHY*

Mission is the driving reason why you do what you do. When was the last time you considered why you do what you do? I'm not talking about why you do the little things, like brush your teeth or get to school on time. I'm asking you about what drives the theme of your life. If you were to share a few words that best define your drive, your *why*, what would they be?

I asked this question to a group of students at a conference after sharing how my sons explain their driving *why* as being "Strong, Brave, and of great Courage." Since the time my sons were small, the brothers have described their strength, bravery, and courage by saying they are "made of mettle." Not the metallic metal like iron or steel, but rather the character trait of mettle—"the measure of a person's determination and strength to carry on, no matter the situation, in a spirited and resilient way." One of the students in the audience raised their hand and said, "I don't know why I

do life each day. Really, all I'm hoping for is that today will be a slightly better repeat of yesterday. How did your sons decide their mission, their why, was to be strong, brave, and courageous?"

"They were told they were," I replied. "Not in a forceful 'I'm telling you' kind of way. Instead, they loved hearing they were Strong, Brave, and of great Courage because one of their favorite people believed in them and told them so, all the time."

SPEAK IT SO

When the boys were young, we lived in a small town just a mile south of the US–Canada border. Across the street from our home was a sweets shop owned by a good friend. Originally from Georgia, she held tight to the southern tradition of greeting people with a smile and the title of Mr. or Ms. to dress up their first name. She called me Mr. Jonathan, my wife Ms. Erica, and our sons by fun bug-related nicknames. And she really liked it when we called her Ms. Jennie.

Ms. Jennie's sweets shop was understandably our sons' favorite place to go. She served fresh-popped kettle corn, specialty candies, and lots of chocolate. Basically, everything our boys loved. Sweet candy served by an even sweeter lady.

During one very memorable Saturday afternoon visit to Ms. Jennie's, our son Reed had a meltdown on the floor of the candy store. He hadn't gotten the treat he wanted and thought a nuclear-powered temper tantrum might change things. Little did he know how right he was, just not in the way he had imagined.

Sprawled out on the floor with fake tears and very real screams pouring from his face, he made his displeasure known to all the customers. In an attempt to correct my son's bad behavior, I began to

scold him by saying, "Reed! Get up off the floor. You are embarrassing yourself." Truth was, he felt just fine down there polishing the floor with his fake tears. I was the embarrassed one. "Get up. Get up right now," I commanded. Taking hold of his arm, I attempted to lift him to his feet. Except he had taken on the consistency of a wet noodle and easily slipped from my grasp, back into a pile on the floor. So I tried again. "That's it, young man. You are in trouble. We are going home, and you'll be in time-out!"

That changed nothing.

From behind me, I heard Ms. Jennie speak up. "There's a better way," she said in her calm Georgian voice. "Reed, Reed, honey. Look at me." Kneeling on the floor, she locked eyes with the rebellious child and said the words none of us would forget.

"Reed. Look at me. This is not the way a strong, brave, and courageous boy acts. No, absolutely not. You are much better than this. You are Strong, Brave, and of great Courage, boy. Now say it with me. 'I am Strong, Brave, and of great Courage.' Good. Now say it with me again. This time kneel beside me. 'I am Strong, Brave, and of great Courage.' Very good. One more time. Except I want to see how tall you are. Stand up and say it with me again. 'I am Strong, Brave, and of great Courage!' Yes, you are. Yes sir."

With that, my son began to march around her shop like a proud lion. With flexed arms and all traces of whining gone, he proclaimed to all that he was Strong, Brave, and of great Courage. Proud of his attitude change and total transformation in behavior, I picked Reed up and gave him a hug.

"How did you do that?" I asked. As a young father, I was working on my parenting skills, and I figured Ms. Jennie knew a few child-rearing secrets I could use to be a better dad.

"I told him the truth. The truth he needed to lift himself up. I told him what he should have heard you say. Instead, you went straight to his failures. You told him he was an embarrassment, in trouble, and

had to spend time alone. I gave him a way to be better. If he chose to be better." Ms. Jennie continued, "Now, let's say it again."

Looking at my son, I expected him and Ms. Jennie to repeat the words to each other. You know, just to set the message a little deeper in Reed. But no. Instead, Ms. Jennie reached out and poked me in the chest. "You too, Mr. Catherman. You say them too."

Ouch! She used my last name. She was serious.

"Yes ma'am," I replied as I stood up straight. With my son held in my arms, I looked Reed in the eyes as we restated the affirming words together. "I am Strong, Brave, and of great Courage."

"You share those words with him every day," Ms. Jennie instructed me. "Every day both your boys need to hear you tell them they are Strong, Brave, and of great Courage. You must speak it so, and you must show them how to make it so. Every single day. Speak it so."

So I did. Every day since Ms. Jennie first said it, my sons have heard me tell them, "You are Strong, Brave, and of great Courage." When we learned that the character trait *mettle* wrapped strength, bravery, and courage all into one, we adopted the word as our own. We even created our own logo with an anvil in the center. The design includes the statement "Made of Mettle—Strength, Bravery, Courage."

The driving reason why my sons do what they do is because of the character traits they believe are important for them to live with purpose.

Strength—the ability to make a positive contribution greater than what is expected in return.

Bravery—the ability to confront pain, danger, or intimidation *without* fear.

+ Courage—the ability to undertake an overwhelming difficulty or pain despite fear.

= Mettle—the measure of a person's determination and strength to carry on, no matter the situation, in a spirited and resilient way.

Are they perfect at it? No. Remember, nobody is perfect. They struggle with the same things all people in Generation Z have to work through. But they know that their mission—the *why* they do what they do—gives their life purpose. Most of the time. When their mission is clear, they get out of bed in the morning, put two feet on the floor, and live in a way that makes each day better than the last—on purpose.

Reed applies his strength, bravery, and courage to help people by advocating for acceptance, respect, and equality despite our differences. His brother, Cole, applies his strength, bravery, and courage to create and work with innovative, competitive, and loyal teams. As their father, I'm excited to see how they apply their mission to their education, work, family, and fun in the years to come.

How would you describe your *mission*, your *why*? What words would you select to help drive you forward each day?

Maybe it's a single word like Mettle or string of words like Strength, Bravery, and Courage. Perhaps your mission is found in the lyrics of a song or in a quote you read. Make up your statement or pick a preexisting one that you find truly inspiring. It's up to you. Just make sure your mission, your *why*, is personal and meaningful.

CONSIDER THIS:

The most successful companies in the world believe in their mission statement. One such company is Nike. Do you know their mission? Spoiler alert. It's not "Just Do It." Nike's corporate mission statement is "To bring inspiration and innovation to every athlete* in the world." See the asterisk after the word *athlete*? Nike believes that "if you have a body, you are an athlete."[1]

YOUR TURN:

1. What words would you use to describe your drive, your *why*?

   - _____
   - _____
   - _____
   - _____
   - _____

2. If you were to ask the people in your life, "What few words best describe my mission, my *why*?" what do you think they would say?

Name: Their Words about Your *Why*:

1. _____   _____

2. _____   _____

3. _____   _____

4. _____   _____

5. _____   _____

Chapter 17

GOALS DEFINE YOUR *WHAT*

Goals define *what* you need to do to make your mission and vision your reality. The power of goals is they move you from where you are now (point A) to where you want to be in the future (point B) within a measurable time frame. One of the best ways to convert your "I wish I could" aspirations into "I'm doing it" goals is to make the process well worth your time. **TIME**, to be exact. Setting and accomplishing your goals makes having the TIME of your life possible. Accomplishing your goals is where your desire to *live with purpose* meets the steps required to make it your reality.

Think It

Think about what matters most to you. What are your highest priorities and greatest aspirations? What are you doing about what matters most to you that moves you from where you are today to where you want to be in the future? Think

about both your *vision's where* and *mission's why* for the short-term and long-term gains you would like to experience.

Vision—A clear mental picture of a desirable future.

Mission—The driving reason why you do what you do.

Ink It

Write your goals down. Start with where you are today in relation to where you want to be in the future. This can be difficult because you may not have truly considered the distance between point A (where you are today) and point B (where you want to be in the future). Not to mention, how long the goal is going to take to accomplish. Here are some examples of the difference between aspirations and specific, achievable goals.

IS IT A GOAL?

No. Not a goal.	Yes! It's a goal.
To spend more time with family.	I will work with my family to move from random family time to one night a week reserved for family, starting the first of next month.
To get better grades.	Every Tuesday and Thursday, I will attend lunch block math tutoring, turn in all my late assignments, and complete any optional extra credit until my grade rises from a low C to a high B.
To save money.	I will go from no money in savings to $50 a paycheck automatic transfer to my savings account, starting next pay period.

No. Not a goal.	Yes! It's a goal.
To get into shape.	Between next week and my birthday in six months, I will exercise for one hour, at the gym, every other day.
To eat better.	Following a heart-healthy, portions-appropriate meal plan, I will cook dinner at home five of seven days a week, starting next Monday.
To get out of debt.	Starting the first of the month, I will budget double payments until my car loan is paid off in two years.

Map It

Once you have your specific, achievable goals written down, decide what action steps you need to take to get started and stay motivated. For instance, the goal to exercise every other day for one hour, at the gym, for the next six months.

- ☐ Action Step 1. Find a gym within five minutes of my house.
- ☐ Action Step 2. Go into the gym, take a guided tour of the facility, and purchase a membership.
- ☐ Action Step 3. Make three appointments with a personal trainer to set a realistic workout plan that will work for me.
- ☐ Action Step 4. Scope out appropriate workout clothes and purchase myself a couple sets of gym clothes.
- ☐ Action Step 5. Reserve the days and times on my calendar for "Gym Time."

Check off each box once the action step has been completed.

Earn It

Now it's time to put your goals into action. Knowing the specifics of where you are today in relation to where you want to be in the future is a good start. Next, how will you track your progress? Do you need to see your progress on an old-school refrigerator chart or is there a new-school digital app for that? How will you celebrate successfully making progress along the way to your ultimate goal? And maybe most important, who will hold you accountable and how often?

Accountability is a big part of accomplishing your goals. In fact, accountability can make the probability of you completing a goal rise from 10 percent to 95 percent. That's a big difference.

Probability of You Completing a Goal

10%—If you just *have* an idea or a goal

25%—If you *consciously decide* you will do it

40%—If you decide *when* you will do it

50%—If you plan *how* you will do it

65%—If you *commit to someone* you will do it

95%—If you have a *specific accountability appointment* with a person you've committed to (also known as an accountability partner)

Think about it—95 percent is almost certainty. If the likelihood of you getting struck by lightning today was 95 percent, would you go outside? No way! If the possibility of you winning a first-place gold medal was 95 percent, would you enter the race? Absolutely! So if you know there

is a 95 percent probability of you successfully accomplishing a goal if you have an accountability partner, who will you ask? But wait. Who you ask to be an accountability partner matters. A true accountability partner will tell you what you need to hear, not just what you want to hear. So choose wisely.

In a way, the secret to success is hidden in accountability. It starts with setting specific and measurable goals. Next, choose an accountability partner who will hold you to a high standard. Then, get to work. Track your progress with easy-to-understand measurements. When you share your progress report with the right accountability partner, your system should pass the three-second rule. If within three seconds of looking at your progress report your accountability partner can see exactly what your goal is, where you started, where you are now, what the next step is, and how much more you have to complete—you have a good system. Kind of like the gauges on a car dashboard. You don't have to study them long to know how much fuel is in the tank, how fast you are going, and if the check engine light is on or not. Your system of reporting goals should be about that easy to understand.

To live with purpose is a remarkable experience. To see clearly a vision for *where* you are going, to believe in *why* your mission is significant, and to know *what* your goals will accomplish is an amazing existence. Wise people know this because their lives serve as living proof. The testimony they present each day is of hope, and the witness they give brings hope to others. An aimless life does not do this. Only those who live with purpose can be certain their life is making a difference.

TOMMY FORD'S FUNERAL

On August 9, 2014, an eighteen-year-old black man named Michael Brown was fatally shot by a white police officer in Ferguson, Missouri. The next day, protesters gathered to mourn Brown's death and march to protest against dissimilar policing practices. In the weeks and months that followed the shooting and subsequent unrest, it became clear to leaders in education, faith communities, and elected officials that a strategy for healing Ferguson's deep racially charged wounds had to include long-term commitments to strengthening their youth.

One action the leadership network implemented was to create opportunities for Ferguson's youth to meet and learn from experts in character, skills, and leadership development. One such figure was actor and comedian Tommy Ford. Best known for his role as "Tommy" on the mid-1990's syndicated sitcom *Martin*, Tommy Ford was a larger-than-life celebrity with a contagious smile and signature laugh. As a Hollywood veteran, Tommy had played parts on TV and film that gave him both the professional credentials and street cred to be admired by fans of all ages and skin colors. So when Tommy Ford appeared in Ferguson in early 2016 to talk with the city's youth and community leadership about the importance of seeing themselves as purposeful, powerful people, his message was well planned and a big hit. This made taking the stage after Tommy a hard act to follow, which is exactly what I had to do.

Thankfully, my session was also well received. After sharing ways to transform youth into confident and capable adults with an audience of teenage guys and their dads, Tommy pulled me aside for a talk. We discussed the importance of boys experiencing rites of passage and learning from older male mentors. Come the end of our conversation, the actor-turned-producer invited me to Atlanta, Georgia, to participate in a documentary film he was producing

titled *Through My Lens*. The project would follow thirty inner-city youth involved in bullying. Some had been aggressors, others victims. Tommy would provide the young men with mentors and training to become amateur filmmakers capable of capturing and examining the complicated world of bullying as it relates to urban populations. Together they would attend sixteen weekly manhood-empowerment workshops with the goal of giving the guys the opportunity to practice the life skills and character traits they would need to break free from negative cycles and stereotypes. Tommy asked if I would come help him teach the guys a few simple tasks that would test and challenge how they saw themselves and strengthen their resolve to find real purpose in life. When I asked Tommy how "simple," he smiled and said, "Hammer-and-nail simple." So that's exactly what we did.

It wasn't long before I was driving to Atlanta equipped with a load of 2x4 lumber, a jobsite count of hammers, and a large box of nails. An hour after pulling into town, I joined Tommy on set, met his production crew, and got ready to film. With cameras capturing our every angle, Tommy introduced me to the guys and their mentors before we set into pounding some nails. I wish you could have seen it. A couple dozen guys standing there in a group, each holding a carpenter's framing hammer, and not one willing to admit he didn't know how to swing it. Sure, anyone can hold a hammer. But it becomes obvious very fast who has a handle on the skill required to strike a nail square on the head. A few guys choked way up on the wooden handle and cautiously introduced the hammer to the nail like they were attempting to tap out a message in Morse code. Others held their hammer in two hands and swung it like a bat. More than a couple mis-struck, bent nails shot across the room, followed by a few choice words. Seeing their frustration mounting, Tommy instructed the guys to pause for a moment and pay close attention to some basic instructions. "Don't worry, we'll walk you through it,"

he assured the group. "Hitting a nail square is a lot like life. Practice will make you better, and when you do it right, you can build about anything."

Following a little training and focused practice, the guys' hammer skills improved quickly. Within the hour, they were all landing their swings well and looking ready for the next lesson.

Of course, none of them were equipped to frame up a house by the end of our session, but they had changed perspectives from thinking *can't*, yet faking like they *could*, to knowing they *can*—and being able to prove it in a couple of swings. This is exactly what Tommy had wanted. He knew if the guys could change the way they saw themselves, they could begin to build a better life. After an hour of hammering nails, the guys were confident enough in themselves to say, "That wasn't so difficult. What else you got?"

A few months later, I received a call with some tragic news. My friend Tommy Ford had died. At only fifty-two years old, Tommy's death from a ruptured aneurysm delivered a sad blow to his family, friends, and fans alike. Particularly hard hit were the cast and crew of *Through My Lens*. Tommy's passion project had become his final creative venture, but not before giving the guys involved a new look on the purpose of life.

I had never attended a memorial service for a celebrity prior to Tommy's, so I had no idea what to expect. Thankfully that mid-October day was a sunny and warm one in Atlanta, as thousands of people showed up to pay their respects. While standing in line beside other well-dressed observers, I felt a hand wrap around my upper arm. Turning in surprise, I realized I was being pulled out of line by one of the guys from Tommy's documentary film. He was a large young man whom I had joked with on set about being even bigger than me. "Us tall guys have to stick together," we had agreed during the filming several months before. Now walking away from the long line of people waiting to enter Tommy's memorial

service, he let my arm go and said, "I remember you. You're the 'how to pound a nail' guy, aren't you? You're in the wrong place. Come with me."

I wasn't sure what exactly was happening or where we were going. Still, I agreed and together we walked away from the line. As we approached the corner of the building, he slowed his pace, turned toward me, and stopped.

"Before we go in, I have to tell you something," he said. "You remember the time Tommy had you teach us how to use a hammer? Well, that day changed my life."

He continued as a smile stretched across his face. "When I got home, my mom asked me what I'd learned. I showed her your book *The Manual to Manhood* and how you wrote me the message on the inside cover, 'Skills make you valuable, Character makes you invaluable.' Then I opened to the pages about How to Swing a Hammer. I told her you and Tommy had taught us about different kinds of hammers and that we had practiced pounding in a bunch of nails." His smile turned to a chuckle. "But my mom can't leave anything alone. She said now that I could use a hammer, she had a job for me. Finally, she could have this big, heavy mirror hung on the wall. And you know what, I used the tools you gave us, and I did it. I found a stud in the wall and I hung that mirror. That really made my mom proud of me."

Just prior to leading me through a lineless set of double doors, he choked up a bit. "Before Tommy died, I told him that I'm going to become a carpenter. When he asked me why, I said, because it would bring meaning to my life. Since nobody in our family knows how to fix stuff, we have to pay someone to help us out. Since we don't have much money, nothing gets fixed. When I become a carpenter, I can help people by fixing stuff. People like my mom," he said. "So that's what I want to do with myself. Swing a hammer to help people. I told Tommy and I thought you might want to know too."

With that, he cleared his throat, turned, and walked me into the building. I followed the tall teen down a short hallway, around a corner, and to a door marked VIP room. Turning to face me squarely, he extended his hand to deliver a very confident handshake. With one final "thank you," he opened the door and ushered me in.

There enjoying light snacks and memories of their friend were people I recognized as celebrities who had worked alongside Tommy. Known comedians, musicians, and a couple of pro athletes mixed about in anticipation of being seated for the service.

Feeling like I had stepped into the wrong room, I turned and looked at the young man with what I can only imagine was an expression of pure confusion on my face.

"Am I supposed to be here?" I asked sheepishly. "I don't know what to do."

"Don't worry. I'll walk you through it," he replied. "Us tall guys have to stick together."

> The way that I find my purpose is to change my lens. To change my focus. That is what a lens does. It gives us focus, it gives the right exposure, it gives us a beautiful picture.[1]
>
> —Tommy Ford

CONSIDER THIS:

Our brains love to accomplish goals. When we successfully achieve a goal, small or large, our brain releases a chemical called *dopamine*. This chemical has also been nicknamed the "feel good" neurotransmitter because it does just that—it makes us feel good.

1. Having the TIME of your life will help you see *what* goals are worth pursuing and which are not. How can you convert some of your vague aspirations into specific, achievable goals? Write down some of your aspirations and practice converting them into goals that fit the model: from point A to point B in a specific time frame.

Vague Aspirations: Specific Goals:

1. _____   _____

2. _____   _____

3. _____   _____

4. _____   _____

5. _____   _____

2. Who can you ask to be an accountability partner who will support you in accomplishing your goals?

_____

_____

_____

3. When you do accomplish your specific goals, how will you celebrate in a meaningful way?

_____

_____

_____

4. With clarity in your goal-setting process, do you feel more purposeful in life? If so, how? What do you believe is your purpose at this time in your life?

_____

_____

_____

CONCLUSION

Each year the news publisher *Time* releases a Most Influential Teens list. Alongside the expected names of young industry-managed pop singers, fresh-faced actors, and teen celebrities are some ordinary young people doing some extraordinary things. They range from a youthful entrepreneur who raised nearly $6 million in venture capital to fund his speed-defying drone designs[1] to a UK teen who developed an antibody that can detect early signs of Alzheimer's disease.[2] On the list of no-names now making a big name for themselves are young climate-change activists, rising civil rights leaders, creative artists, innovative white-hat hackers, title-winning athletes, and culinary geniuses. All under the age of twenty.

Time features about twenty-five new young people each year. Each new account of their excellence more impressive than the last. I look forward to watching their stories develop as they grow into adulthood and inherit the world my generation is preparing to pass on to them. Understandably, there isn't enough room in each year's publication for the countless number of young people who are doing great things. Empowered with more and better resources than any generation before, you are truly beginning to change the world in new

and better ways. Unfortunately, the field of options you have to choose from is almost too vast. Sorry, some of that is my generation's fault.

In many ways, we, the premillennium generations, set up your generation for great success. I say this because we made two very significant marks in history to set the scene for your succession. First, we took the big step out of the Industrial Age into the Information Age, also called the Computer Age, Digital Age, or New Media Age. Your parents and grandparents moved rapidly through the transition between a world fueled by textile, wood, brick, and steel industries into global trading on products powered by information technology. Second, we kind of trashed the place and a lot of people along the way. We polluted the water and air. We created and successfully marketed overprocessed convenience foods. We made delivering the horrors of war far more efficient and effective than ever before. These are just a few of the scars we leave for your inheritance. If we can't fix these issues before we go, you will have to.

The new era we created and the old sins we leave behind are going to be a tall order for your generation to handle. It's our responsibility to ready you for tomorrow, yet we have no idea what the world will actually look like in a few years. One thing we can be certain of is, if we set you up to do the same as we did, yet expect your generation to produce different results, we're the wrong kind of crazy. All new insights begin with a break from old ways of looking at things. The principles and models we have considered in *Becoming the Next Great Generation* require us to rethink how your generation will steward what we failed to.

Living and sharing ways to cross the growing gap between generations should be one of our highest priorities.

As we *Build Bridges*, *Practice Stewardship before Leadership*, *Transform Raw Talents into Valued Strengths*, and *Live with Purpose*, we will grow closer together, and I truly believe we will see something remarkable take place. Those of us born way back in the 1900s will continue to discover and become our greatest potential while we witness you do and be even better than us as you become the *Next Great Generation*.

NOTES

Personal Message to Readers

1. "Here's to the Crazy Ones," Think Different ad campaign, Apple, 1997, http://www.thecrazyones.it/spot-en.html.
2. "Here's to the Crazy Ones."

Introduction

1. "DJ Jazzy Jeff and Fresh Prince," RIAA Searchable Database, Recording Industry Association of America, https://www.riaa.com/gold -platinum/?tab_active=default-award&se=parents+just+don%27t+ understand#search_section, accessed Nov. 10, 2008.
2. "The Source's Top 100 Rap Albums of All Time," rateyourmus ic.com, https://rateyourmusic.com/list/Tempetz/the_sources_top_100 _rap_albums_of_all_time/.
3. Sean Smith, "Will Smith: Hollywood's Most Powerful Actor?" *Newsweek*, April 8, 2007, https://www.newsweek.com/will-smith-holly woods-most-powerful-actor-97639.
4. John Burman, "Hollywood's Most Valuable Actors," *Forbes*, February 10, 2009, https://www.forbes.com/2009/02/10/forbes-star-currency-busi ness-media-star-currency-09_0210_star_currency.html#7224d4e2361b.

Chapter 1 The Space between Us

1. "A database of 50 years of FORTUNE's list of America's largest corporations," *Fortune 500*, http://archive.fortune.com/magazines/fortune /fortune500_archive/full/1965/.
2. Gordan E. Moore, "Cramming More Components onto Integrated Circuits," *Electronics* 38, no. 8 (April 19, 1965).

3. Carolyn Henson, "SMS Celebrates 20th Anniversary," *Wall Street Journal*, Dec. 3, 2012, https://blogs.wsj.com/tech-europe/2012/12/03/sms-celebrates-20th-anniversary/.

4. Whitney Johnson, "Why Today's Teens Are More Entrepreneurial Than Their Parents," *Harvard Business Review*, May 25, 2015, https://hbr.org/2015/05/why-todays-teens-are-more-entrepreneurial-than-their-parents.

Chapter 2 New Normal

1. Michael Dimock, "Defining Generations: Where Millennials End and Post-Millennials Begin," Pew Research Center, March 1, 2018, http://www.pewresearch.org/fact-tank/2018/03/01/defining-generations-where-millennials-end-and-post-millennials-begin/.

2. Thomas Aichner and Paolo Coletti, "Customers' Online Shopping Preferences in Mass Customization," *Journal of Direct, Data, and Digital Marketing Practice* 15 (2013): 20, https://doi.org/10.1057/dddmp.2013.34.

Chapter 3 Crossing Over

1. "Resident Population in the United States in 2017," Statista, https://www.statista.com/statistics/797321/us-population-by-generation/.

Chapter 4 Rethinking Leadership

1. Brandon Busteed, "The School Cliff: Student Engagement Drops with Each School Year," Gallup, Jan. 7, 2013.

2. Rasmus Hougaard, "The Real Crisis in Leadership," *Forbes*, Sept. 9, 2018, https://www.forbes.com/sites/rasmushougaard/2018/09/09/the-real-crisis-in-leadership/#2fd73e1b3ee4.

3. Gallup, State of The American Workplace Report 2017, page 19.

4. Falon Fatemi, "What's Your Strategy for Attracting Generation Z," *Forbes*, March 31, 2018, https://www.forbes.com/sites/falonfatemi/2018/03/31/whats-your-strategy-for-attracting-generation-z/#3c2fd0dd6cad.

Chapter 5 Membership

1. Toshiko Kaneda and Carl Haub, "How Many People Have Ever Lived on Earth?" March 9, 2018, PRB, https://www.prb.org/howmanypeoplehaveeverlivedonearth/.

2. K. D. Williams, "Ostracism," *Annual Review of Psychology* 58 (2007): 425–52.

3. N. I. Eisenberger, M. D. Lieberman, and K. D. Williams, "Does Rejection Hurt? An fMRI Study of Social Exclusion," *Science* 302 (2003): 290–92.

4. S. J. Karau and K. D. Williams, "Social Loafing: A Meta-Analytic Review and Theoretical Integration," *Journal of Personality and Social Psychology* 65 (1993): 681–706.

Chapter 6 Stewardship

1. Mike Rowe, "The Girl Who Feeds the Hungry," *Returning the Favor*, season 2, episode 22, https://www.facebook.com/ReturningTheFavor/videos/2084159171855342/.

2. Mackenzie Hinson, personal interview with author, July 22, 2019.

3. Global Issues Overview, United Nations, https://www.un.org/en/sections/issues-depth/global-issues-overview/.

Chapter 7 Leadership

1. Steve Denning, "The Best of Peter Drucker," *Forbes*, Aug. 9, 2014.

2. Christianity Today International/LEADERSHIP 17, no. 4 (Fall 1996): 54.

3. Peter F. Drucker, *Management: Tasks, Responsibilities, Practices* (New York: HarperBusiness, 1993), 463.

4. Stephen R. Covey, "Voices on Leadership: Stephen R. Covey," *Washington Post*, July 17, 2008, http://www.washingtonpost.com/wp-dyn/content/discussion/2008/07/16/DI2008071602427.html?noredirect=on.

5. Stephen R. Covey, *The 8th Habit: From Effectiveness to Greatness* (New York: Free Press, 2005), 98.

6. "Marie Curie (1867–1934): Her Life, Achievements and Legacy," History Extra, https://www.historyextra.com/period/first-world-war/life-of-the-week-marie-curie/.

Chapter 8 View from 30,000 Feet

1. "Many Trophies for Tossers in State Tourney," *Evening Independent*, Feb. 8, 1922, https://newspaperarchive.com/sports-clipping-feb-08-1922-1129748/.

Chapter 9 Talent

1. Marcus Buckingham and Donald O. Clifton, *Now, Discover Your Strengths* (New York: Free Press, 2001), 29.

Chapter 10 Training

1. "Skill Sets in Nontraditional Careers," Minnesota State CAREERwise, https://careerwise.minnstate.edu/careers/skillsets.html.

2. George Kuh, Ken O'Donnell, and Carol Geary Schneider, "HIPs at Ten," Change, 49:5, 8–16, DOI: 10.1080/00091383.2017.1366805.

3. "Completing College—National—2018," NSC Research Center, Dec. 18, 2018, https://nscresearchcenter.org/signaturereport16/.

Chapter 11 Timing

1. Lexico, s.v. "perfect (adj.)," https://www.lexico.com/definition/perfect.

2. "Stefan Comăneci, Nadia's mother: 'I am proud of her!'" Libertatea, http://www.libertatea.ro/sport/alte-sporturi/stefania-comaneci-mama -nadiei-sunt-mandra-de-ea-665179.

3. "Human to Hero: Nadia Comaneci—Olympic Gymnastics' First Perfect 10," CNN, April 3, 2012, https://www.cnn.com/2012/04/03/sport /olympics-nadia-comaneci/index.html.

4. Malcolm Gladwell, *Outliers: The Story of Success* (New York: Little, Brown and Co., 2008): 38–39.

5. Malcolm Gladwell, "Hi, I'm Malcolm Gladwell, author of . . ." (archived), https://www.reddit.com/r/IAmA/comments/2740ct/hi_im_mal colm_gladwell_author_of_the_tipping/chx6ku3/?context=8&depth=9.

6. "Human to Hero: Nadia Comaneci."

7. Sam Rega, "Professional Video Game Players Practice Up to 17 Hours a Day Because 'Brute Force Number of Hours' Is the Only Way to Improve," *Business Insider*, April 29, 2016, video, 1:58, https://www.business insider.com/how-pro-video-game-players-spend-money-2016-4.

Chapter 12 Treasure

1. Robert Frost, "The Road Not Taken," first published in 1915.

2. "Americans Satisfied with Number of Friends, Closeness of Friendships," Gallup, March 5, 2004, https://news.gallup.com/poll/10891/ameri cans-satisfied-number-friends-closeness-friendships.aspx.

3. C. W. Headley, "Hew Study Claims the Average American Has This Many Friends," Ladders, May 14, 2019, https://www.theladders.com /career-advice/new-study-claims-that-the-average-american-has-this -many-friends.

Chapter 13 Strength

1. "U.S. Skills Gap," SkillsUSA, https://www.skillsusa.org/about/why -career-technical-education/stem-and-cte-alignment/u-s-skills-gap/.

2. "U.S. Skills Gap."

3. "Stats and Facts on Leadership and Management," Lead through Strengths, https://leadthroughstrengths.com/stats/.

Chapter 14 One-of-One

1. "How Millennials and Generation Z Are Redefining Work," The Change Generation Report 2017, Lovell Corporation, https://www.lovell corporation.com/the-change-generation-report/.

Chapter 16 Mission Defines Your *Why*

1. "Our Mission," Nike.com, https://about.nike.com.

Chapter 17 Goals Define Your *What*

1. Tommy Ford, "Tommy Ford Presents . . . *Through My Lens* Teaser," YouTube, May 27, 2016, www.youtube.com/watch?v=dmDyxmY1wFs.

Conclusion

1. "The 30 Most Influential Teens of 2016," *Time*, October 19, 2016, http://time.com/4532104/most-influential-teens-2016/.

2. "The 30 Most Influential Teens of 2017," *Time*, November 3, 2017, http://time.com/5003930/most-influential-teens-2017/.

Jonathan Catherman is the author of the international best-selling book *The Manual to Manhood*. He coauthored the bestseller *The Manual to Middle School* with his sons, Reed and Cole, and *The Girls' Guide to Conquering Life* and *The Girls' Guide to Conquering Middle School* with his wife, Erica. An award-winning cultural strategist and leading education trainer specializing in the character and leadership development of youth, Jonathan speaks worldwide about the principles and strengths that empower greatness in children, teens, and young adults. Jonathan and his family live in North Carolina where they founded and direct the 1M Mentoring Foundation. Learn more at www.thecathermans.com.

CONNECT WITH

JONATHAN CATHERMAN!

Author, Speaker, Consultant, Creator

To learn more about Jonathan Catherman's
speaking, consulting, and mentoring, visit

WWW.THECATHERMANS.COM

The Practical Advice Guys Need to Become
CONFIDENT AND CAPABLE

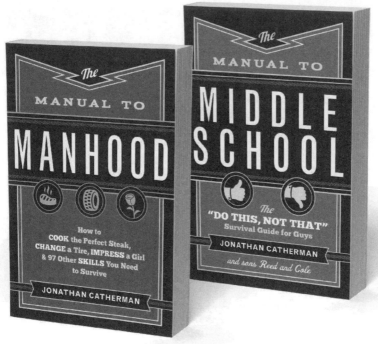

These practical illustrated guides contain valuable information and direction for some of life's trickiest moments. Set yourself up for success with instructions on almost everything a guy needs to know.

The Practical Advice Young Women Need to Become

PREPARED, CONFIDENT, AND SUCCESSFUL

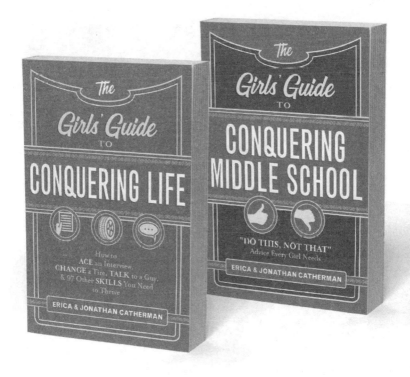

These practical illustrated guides contain valuable information and direction for some of life's trickiest moments. Set yourself up for success and be ready to handle what life throws at you.

Books by Jonathan Catherman

The Manual to Manhood
The Manual to Middle School
Guiding the Next Great Generation
Becoming the Next Great Generation

With Erica Catherman

The Girls' Guide to Conquering Life
The Girls' Guide to Conquering Middle School

Becoming
THE NEXT
GREAT
GENERATION